Saving Myself

The Quintessential Guide to Building a Budget, Getting Out of Debt and Living Your Dream Life

JO BAKER

First published by Ultimate World Publishing 2024
Copyright © 2024 Jo Baker

ISBN

Paperback: 978-1-922714-43-5
Ebook: 978-1-922714-44-2

Jo Baker has asserted her rights under the Copyright, Designs and Patents Act 1988 to be identified as the author of this work. The information in this book is based on the author's experiences and opinions. The publisher specifically disclaims responsibility for any adverse consequences which may result from use of the information contained herein. Permission to use information has been sought by the author. Any breaches will be rectified in further editions of the book.

All rights reserved. No part of this publication may be reproduced, stored in or introduced into a retrieval system, or transmitted in any form, or by any means (electronic, mechanical, photocopying, recording or otherwise) without the prior written permission of the author. Any person who does any unauthorised act in relation to this publication may be liable to criminal prosecution and civil claims for damages. Enquiries should be made through the publisher.

Cover design: Ultimate World Publishing
Layout and typesetting: Ultimate World Publishing
Editor: Rebecca Low

Ultimate World Publishing
Diamond Creek,
Victoria Australia 3089
www.writeabook.com.au

Testimonials

So often, we pick up a book with the best of plans to improve our lives, but by page 15, the author has lost us and bored us to tears, not Jo's *Saving Myself*. From the introduction, you feel like you're curled up on the couch with a trusted friend who actually wants you to succeed and has you engaged the whole time. She teaches you how to take control of that one thing most of us all struggle with: money. I implore you to read this book. You'll be amazed by how it can help you become a Queen of Choices and no longer a Hot Money Mess.

Suskia
Single Parent & Full Time Professional (Once a Hot Money Mess, now on my way to a Queen of Choices)

Bestselling author Jo Baker's latest book is filled with inspiration and wisdom drawn from personal experience. Jo shares the story of her own financial transformation as she guides women to tap into their innate strength, resilience, and determination to create a truly empowering financial future for themselves. With heart, insight, and practical advice, this is a must-read for any woman looking to rewrite her financial story.

Therese Cassidy
Founder of www.updateyourcv.com

I love Jo's explanation of the relationship of this book with mental, financial and general health and well-being. This is particularly important for those of us in the neurodivergent world. Clear, concise directions with inspirational tips. Thank you.

Lorraine Brookes

Saving Myself

Saving Myself is an inspiring and uplifting guide for any woman who's ready to take charge of her financial future. Jo shares personal stories and offers practical advice, making the process of managing money feel not only achievable but empowering. This book has the power to transform both how you approach your finances and how you see yourself. It's a must-read for women ready to embrace their financial strength and build a life of freedom and choice.

Sandi Fulcher
Executive Assistant for the
CEO of WomenCAN Australia

A must-read for women ready to take control of their finances in a way that feels supportive and achievable. With practical steps and inspiring stories, it empowers you to rewrite your financial narrative and step into your true potential.

Kate Thorp
Change and Transformation Leader

From the very beginning, *Saving Myself* spoke to me. It was an easy-to-read format with practical tips and step-by-step instructions. Jo values a positive mindset, which I love, and offers genuine support, wisdom, and literacy. This book will help you shift your perspective and reclaim your power. It will truly change your life.

Kristen Ableson
Equine Leadership Facilitator, Author, Physiotherapist

Saving Myself is an inspiring and practical guide for women ready to shift their mindset around money. Jo writes with compassion and clarity, making the complex world of finance feel simple and approachable. This empowering book blends wisdom with

Testimonials

actionable advice, offering women the confidence and tools they need to take charge of their financial destiny and achieve true financial freedom.

Lana Hall
Organisational Change Management & Transformation Leader

Saving Myself by Jo Baker is a transformative read that inspires you to break free from the chains of debt and embrace your dream life. With relatable anecdotes and actionable strategies, Jo empowers you to take charge of your financial journey. This book is a must-read for anyone ready to reclaim their future and live life on their own terms!

Maddy
Hairdresser

Not only is this book practical and full of wisdom, but there is a hidden ingredient. The love, which emanates from Jo's heart when she connects with a common, yet difficult problem women of the modern world face, is mammoth. Her words and guidance are of immense value.

Ludmila Basa
Bio-Energy Healer

To every woman who has ever doubted herself.

This is for you—the one who is ready to rewrite her story, take charge of her future, and embrace the power that's been within her all along.

May this book be your guide as you step confidently into the life you deserve—one of financial freedom, choice, and unwavering self-belief.

It's Never Too Late

"For what it's worth, it's never too late, or in my case, too early to be whoever you want to be. There's no time limit, stop whenever you want. You can change or stay the same, there are no rules to this thing. We can make the best or the worst of it. I hope you make the best of it. And I hope you see things that startle you. I hope you feel things you never felt before. I hope you meet people with a different point of view. I hope you live a life you're proud of. If you find that you're not, I hope you have the courage to start all over again."

~ F. Scott Fitzgerald ~

Contents

Testimonials	iii
Dedication	vii
It's Never Too Late	ix
A Note to You, The Reader	1
Hello, Hello, Hello!	7
My Journey of Financial Empowerment	17
Chapter One: Set Up Your Success	23
Chapter Two: Begin Your Business	43
Chapter Three: Shift Your Story	53
Chapter Four: Manage Your Mindset	61
Chapter Five: Nail Your Numbers	71
Chapter Six: Build Your Budget	89
Chapter Seven: Demolish Your Debt	103
Chapter Eight: Nourish Your Nest Egg	113
Chapter Nine: Hone Your Habits	123
Chapter Ten: Take Your Time	139
Chapter Eleven: Live Your Life	149
Chapter Twelve: Fashion Your First-Aid Kit	159
Conclusion	167
Do Not Allow Your Fire To Go Out	173
Your Journey Continues	175
About the Author	177
Acknowledgements	179

A Note to You, The Reader

If you've picked up this book (thank you for that, by the way), it's likely because you're ready for something different. Maybe you've been feeling stuck or dissatisfied, wondering if there's more out there for you. Let me reassure you.

Yes, you can change your life. It may not happen overnight, but I promise, step by step, you'll get there. Even if it feels overwhelming right now, you have what it takes to make this change.

Yes, you can find happiness again. Whatever has been holding you back, be it fear, uncertainty, or just the weight of routine, doesn't have to define your future. Joy, fulfilment, and excitement are waiting for you on the other side.

Yes, you'll come out of this as a stronger, more confident version of yourself. The journey might feel challenging at times, but you'll be amazed by what you're capable of. The woman you'll become will surprise you with her resilience, bravery, and dedication to living life on her own terms.

How do I know this?

Because I've been in a place of uncertainty, feeling stuck in situations that didn't align with the life I truly wanted. I've faced challenges, made difficult decisions, and found myself starting over more times than I can count. But with each new beginning, I learnt more about who I am and what I'm capable of.

I've picked up the pieces of my life and rebuilt it—more than once—into something I'm incredibly proud of. I've turned dreams into reality, creating a life that once felt out of reach. And now, I'm here to share what I've learnt with you.

The ideas I teach in this book aren't just concepts; they're the principles that helped me and countless others transform our lives. I'm living proof that you can make a change, no matter where you're starting from. And so are the women I've worked with, who have made the decision to step into their power and create a life they love.

If you're holding this book in your hands, you've already taken the first step. The simple act of choosing to seek out change means you're on the path toward something new. All it takes is 10 minutes a day to start shifting your situation and creating real transformation.

The goal isn't about building wealth for wealth's sake or competing with anyone else. This is about creating the financial freedom to live life on your terms—to feel secure, empowered, and in control. Your life is yours to shape now. It's time to leave the past behind and write a new chapter as the heroine of your own story.

You don't have to relive the struggles of yesterday. The hardest part is already behind you. Now, it's time to focus on what's ahead—the strength, joy, and possibilities waiting for you as you begin this new journey.

My hope for you is that by reading this book, you'll discover your strength, courage, and power to create the life you've always dreamt of.

Change is Scary

This book is your golden ticket to a transformative journey, one that's set to shake up how you see yourself, your money, and your life. And let's be real—change can be a bit like jumping into a lake when you don't know how deep it is. It can be daunting. We can find it challenging to embrace new ideas, let alone welcome them with open arms.

As you complete the carefully outlined actions in this book, you might catch yourself being drawn back to the comfort of the things you already know. You might find yourself negotiating with your current reality, wondering to yourself, "Is it really that bad?"—even if that reality is quietly sucking the joy from your life.

Here's the nitty-gritty: all you need is to commit to learning and, even more crucially, doing. Yep, you heard it right—don't skip the doing part. I'll say it louder for the ones in the back: DO NOT SKIP THE DOING PART. Reading this book won't magically transform your life; it's the bold moves you make that carry the magic. Push through those niggling feelings and worries, take tangible steps, and follow the roadmap waiting at the end of each chapter.

It's fair to say that change can give you a twinge of anxiety or a wave of uncertainty, but within the pages of this book, you'll unveil its undeniable potential. The good news is that we're not catapulting into the unknown in one giant leap. Instead, we're taking measured, manageable steps to ensure you don't feel like you're drowning in information. You can set your own pace and move towards a future with possibilities.

In the wise words of Lao Tzu,

> "Every journey begins with a single step."

Today marks that first stride—a purposeful move towards reclaiming your life. Are you ready for this exciting adventure?

Financial Advice Disclaimer

Before we begin this fantastic journey together, let me lay it all out on the table. I'm not your typical financial guru or numbers wizard. And I'm absolutely not a financial planner, accountant, or adviser.

I'm Jo Baker, your dedicated women's empowerment coach, here to guide extraordinary women like you through their personal money adventures.

Now, this is the bit that the lawyers said I had to say so that none of us gets into trouble.

Important Notice: Not Professional Advice

This book, *Saving Myself*, is intended to provide general information and insights into financial empowerment. Jo Baker, the author, is a women's empowerment coach, not a licensed financial advisor or professional.

A Note to You, The Reader

The content presented in this book is for educational and illustrative purposes only. It doesn't constitute financial, investment, or legal advice. The information shared is based on the author's experiences, research, and observations and may not be suitable for every individual.

Readers are encouraged to consider their financial situation and consult a qualified financial professional before making any financial decisions. Each individual's circumstances are unique, and what works for one person may not be suitable for another.

Jo Baker and any associated entities are not responsible for any financial losses, damages, or consequences resulting from the use or reliance upon the information provided in this book. Readers should exercise their discretion and judgment when applying the principles and strategies discussed.

By reading this book, you acknowledge and agree that the author and any associated entities are not liable for any financial decisions or actions you may take based on the information presented herein.

So, what does that mean for those of us who aren't legal eagles?

General Goodies: The information nestled within these pages is more like a general roadmap than a personalised GPS. It's designed to light up your money path, but remember, everyone's journey is unique.

Your Needs, Your Power: Take a moment to ponder if what you're reading aligns with your distinct needs. Think of it like trying on shoes; not every pair fits perfectly.

Saving Myself

Professional Love: If you find yourself in need of some financial TLC, consider seeking the advice of a professional financial adviser. They're like the fairy godmothers of money, waving their wands to create a plan just for you.

Liability Limbo: While I'm here to sprinkle financial empowerment like confetti, it's important to note that I, Jo Baker, and all the legal entities in the mix aren't held responsible for any financial rollercoasters. Whether it's due to a slip-up or something else, we've got to keep it real.

Remember, this journey is all about empowerment, and you've got the magic wand to make decisions that best suit your financial fairy tale.

Hello, Hello, Hello!

Yay! You're here!

Welcome to a journey that's not just about money but about unlocking the power within you. You've just opened the door to a transformative experience where, together, we'll rewrite narratives and rediscover the incredible strength that resides within you.

Have you ever felt stifled by other people's expectations, silenced about money, or nudged to stay small? Have you ever been told, "That's a nice idea, honey, but let's be realistic. Money matters are better left to the experts, don't you think?"

You can hear the patronising tone, can't you?!

Perhaps you've felt like you're not good at maths, or maybe the thoughts of being too old to start or too young to begin have crossed your mind.

You might have even considered there's no point in worrying about it now because it's too late anyway.

Others might say it's too early to start because, after all, you have years left before you truly need to worry about money.

But let me tell you, the best time to empower yourself financially is always now.

This book is your gentle guide, written by someone who has experienced all those things and more who refused to be confined by anyone's limitations.

Now, let's shine a light on the not-so-secret elephant in the room—money. For too long, we've been handed scripts dictating that 'nice girls' don't discuss money or it's not 'ladylike' to talk about wealth. Society might whisper or perhaps suggest that financial matters are best left to 'others.' Some might argue that women should focus on more 'suitable' topics. But let me assure you, breaking free from these outdated scripts is the key to unlocking your financial empowerment.

So, let me share a revolutionary truth with you: not only can we talk about money, but we can also master it! Enter stage right—*Saving Myself*, your quintessential guide to financial empowerment.

Now, I want to make something really clear. This book isn't about amassing opulent wealth. We're not talking about jet-setting around the world in your private jet, drinking out of diamond-encrusted goblets filled with the world's finest champagne (well, not unless that's what you really want). No! It's about creating your financial foundation and using it as a launchpad for life's endless possibilities.

So, why continue reading? Because this is your chance to step into a world where financial empowerment isn't a lofty dream; it's your tangible reality. In fact, it's your birthright!

In the upcoming chapters, we'll unravel the myth that money management is an insurmountable challenge.

Consider this an invitation to kick those money worries out of the closet and give your finances a makeover that'll have them striking a pose in the mirror every day.

Saving Myself isn't just a book; it's your confidante, your trusted ally for breaking free from the chains of outdated expectations. It's for women who dare to dream big, live boldly, and embrace a future free from the chains of financial worry.

Feeling tired of hearing your dreams are too big or your ambitions too audacious? Well, guess what? You're in the right place. Let's begin on this adventure—where money equals choice, and financial stability becomes your reality, allowing you to savour life's indulgences minus guilt.

No more dreams lingering in the dark. It's time for your financial glow-up. Let's waltz down the path to financial stability, one empowered step at a time.

Here's to flipping the script and embracing your financial prowess!

Shattering the Shame and Mystery of Money

In the realm of personal finance, an unspoken veil of shame and mystery has often surrounded women's relationship with money. Society's whispers and expectations have contributed to an environment where openly discussing financial aspirations is met with hesitation. We're going to challenge this narrative and start on a journey of removing the shame and mystery you may feel about your money.

First and foremost, let's dispel the myth that financial well-being is a topic reserved for a select few. As we've just discussed, wealth is a potent source of empowerment. It's not just about accumulating assets; it's about gaining the freedom to make choices that align with our dreams, values, and ambitions. By acknowledging this truth, we liberate ourselves from societal stigmas and pave the way for a healthier, more open dialogue around our financial goals.

It's time for us to embrace financial authenticity, rejecting the notion that discussing money is not a lady-like quality. Every financial journey is unique and filled with triumphs, challenges, and aspirations. By owning our stories and sharing our experiences, we contribute to a collective effort to remove the shame and embarrassment associated with financial matters.

The mystery surrounding money often stems from a lack of understanding. Financial literacy isn't a secret code; it's a key to empowerment. We break down barriers by demystifying the language of finance and fostering an environment where we feel encouraged to educate ourselves. Knowledge becomes the catalyst for change, allowing us to confidently navigate our financial landscapes and make informed decisions aligned with our goals.

Why Now Is The Best Time

Amidst the journey towards financial liberation, the question arises – why now? Why is this moment the opportune time for us to pay attention to our money?

Now is the best time because the narrative is shifting. Society is awakening to the importance of women's financial empowerment, acknowledging that women's dreams, goals, and financial well-being are as significant as any man's. The conversation around money is evolving, making room for diverse voices and perspectives.

Now is the best time because resources and support are more accessible than ever before. The digital age has provided an abundance of information, online communities, and educational platforms that cater specifically to women seeking financial knowledge. The avenues to enhance financial literacy are boundless, from podcasts to webinars and books to conferences.

Now is the best time because the world is recognising the economic influence of women. The acknowledgment of women as powerful contributors to the economy underscores the importance of women being actively engaged in their financial journeys. The moment is ripe for women to step into their financial prowess, not as an afterthought but as integral players in the economic landscape.

Now is the best time because the future is uncertain, and financial preparedness is a form of empowerment. Life is unpredictable, and being financially savvy provides a buffer against unforeseen challenges. By taking charge of their finances now, women can build resilience and create a foundation that withstands the tests of time.

In essence, now is the best time for women to pay attention to their money because the tides are turning, resources are abundant, economic landscapes are evolving, and the journey towards financial liberation is both empowering and essential. This moment isn't just a call to action; it's an invitation to seize the opportunity, break free from old narratives, and craft a future where women stand tall in their financial power.

Now, you might be wondering, "That's great, but how does that apply to me?" Let me share with you why this very moment is the golden opportunity for you to *Save Yourself* financially.

Firstly, let's talk about the power of the present. Time is your secret weapon, and the sooner you start, the more time you have to work your financial magic. Whether you're in your twenties, thirties, forties, fifties like me, or beyond, today is the day to seize control of your financial destiny. Trust me, your future self will be doing a happy dance because of the decisions you make right now.

Secondly, let's address the other elephant in the room—change is a constant, and the financial world is no exception. The sooner you dive into the world of *Saving Myself*, the better equipped you'll be to navigate the twists and turns that inevitably come your way.

And did I mention the satisfaction of seeing your money grow? Starting now means you'll get a front-row seat to witness the fruits of your financial decisions. Imagine watching your savings blossom, debts disappearing into thin air, and your financial confidence soaring higher than ever. It's like a financial garden, and you're the master gardener cultivating a landscape of abundance.

Let's not forget the sweet taste of financial freedom. By starting your journey today, you're paving the way for a future where your money works for you, not the other way around. It's about creating a life where you call the shots, make choices based on what truly matters to you, and enjoy the freedom that comes with being in control of your finances.

Now, I know life can get hectic, and it's tempting to put things off. But here's the real deal – there's no perfect time to start, and waiting for the stars to align might leave you waiting forever. The perfect time is now. Trust me; your future self will be sending you thank-you notes for taking the reins of your financial journey today.

So, if you've been contemplating when to dive into *Saving Myself*, let me tell you, the time is now. Your financial adventure awaits, and the sooner you start, the sooner you'll be strutting down the path to financial empowerment. Let's make today the day you declare, "I'm taking charge of my financial future, and I'm doing it my way!"

New Way of Life

Living as the Queen of Choices is a new way of life. It cuts out all the extraneous noise and activity that goes on in and around us. It simplifies things into three steps.

Step 1: Have a Plan
As Benjamin Franklin says, "If you fail to plan, you plan to fail." And the Queen of Choices loves a good plan. It helps soothe the control freak that lives within her. It takes the ideas out of her head and breathes life into them. It gives her a roadmap to follow as she rebuilds her new life.

Step 2: Create Positive Healthy Habits
A plan without any action is just a plan. A piece of paper with an amazing idea that will fill your heart with joy but never really actualise. Creating positive, healthy habits is like adding a special sauce to your favourite meal. These are the activities or practices you need to do daily, weekly, or monthly to make your plans come to life.

Step 3: Set a Timeframe
With most plans, unless it's something simple that can be done in a day or a week, it will take some time to make them happen.

A lot of us are guilty of giving up on our plans when they don't happen fast enough. However, the plans we're making to create our new future will take time. We're playing the long game. We're achieving our milestones and ticking off items from our to-do lists one step at a time.

The key is this:

A plan plus positive, healthy habits, over time, equals a new way of life.

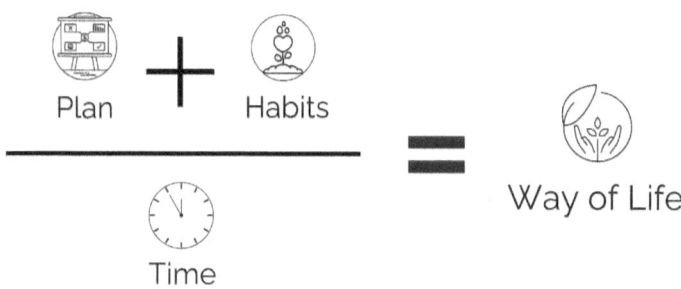

I apply this to everything I do: my finances, holidays, work, goals, and future. And it gets results.

It's Your Turn

At the end of each chapter, you'll see a section called 'It's Your Turn.' This is the 'doing' part of the book.

The last thing I want is for this book to become something you read, identify with, and think there are some clever ideas you could use but then put back on the shelf. Not gonna lie; that would slay me!

Hello, Hello, Hello!

So, take this book out of the 'nice to know' category and put it squarely in the 'I'm doing it' action plan.

Each chapter will end with clearly outlined steps you need to take to create your plan, the habits you need to add the special sauce to, and realistic timeframes so that you can manage your expectations and stop yourself from becoming overwhelmed.

Then, you can begin to reshape your new life, starting with your finances.

My Journey of Financial Empowerment

From Hot Money Mess to the Queen of Choices

Welcome to the chapter of my life that laid the foundation for the person I am today—a self-made woman living life on my own terms. But let's rewind a bit because my journey wasn't always paved with financial triumphs.

There was a time when I was what I lovingly call a "Hot Money Mess." My finances were a chaotic whirlwind, reflecting a time when I simply didn't prioritise money. I lived in blissful ignorance, believing that everything would magically fall into place as long as I was a decent person. I rarely opened my bank statements, choosing instead to shove them into a drawer and never think about them again. My financial strategy? I was just 'winging it.' As weeks turned into months and then years, I found myself stuck in a repetitive cycle of spending and waiting for my payday, completely unaware of where my money was actually going. I believed that if I didn't think about it too much, I wouldn't have to confront my fear.

Looking back, I realise that my situation stemmed from a deeply ingrained belief that focusing on finances wasn't ladylike. I had been conditioned to think that being a 'good girl' meant prioritising relationships and nurturing others over my own financial independence. This belief kept me trapped in a cycle of neglect, where I equated financial literacy with selfishness. I thought that if I focused on money, I would be seen as greedy or materialistic. It felt as though money management was meant for others while I should be busy caring for my family and friends. I never realised that I could embody both kindness and financial savvy at the same time.

The impact of this conditioning was profound for me. I was more likely to avoid risk and hesitate to pursue opportunities, all because I felt I had to conform to the nurturing role I'd been taught to embrace. This fear of stepping outside that role led to many missed opportunities. I felt guilty whenever I considered putting my financial goals first, perpetuating a cycle of dependence that kept me from fully embracing my potential.

Then came a moment that shook me awake. I faced a financial emergency without a safety net, and it hit me hard. I had a stunning realisation that my blissful ignorance had very serious consequences. It was like standing on shaky ground, with the very real threat of falling at any moment. This experience forced me to confront my situation and make a change.

One day, when my kids were little, I was sitting at the dining table, watching them play outside. I've got four children and they were all in the backyard. It was a really hot Sunday in Brisbane, and they had the hose on, running through the water and wetting each other. The kids were laughing and squealing. You know the giggle that kids have when they get really, really excited, and it's contagious, right? It really makes you smile.

My Journey of Financial Empowerment

Their faces were bright red, everything was saturated, and they were having the best time.

I was sitting at my dining table with tears running down my face. Because when I looked at the table, I had four piles of papers. I had a pile of my bank statements, bills, overdue notices, and red letters—these are the final bills they send you before they cut off your power, water, etc. I was one decision away from being homeless. I had four children, and at that moment, I knew that I couldn't keep doing this anymore. I was the closest I had ever been to giving up and moving back in with my parents. Could you imagine? I was 34 years old with four children, knowing that the only solution was to pack up my home and my children and go back to my parents because I couldn't get my financial shit together.

I had just gotten off the phone with a lovely woman at my bank who told me they had declined my request to increase my credit card limit again. I couldn't have any more money. I was already $35,000 in credit card debt, and they couldn't give me another dollar. I had $8.07 in my bank account, and my electricity was about to be cut off.

Have you ever reached a point where you're so sick of your own nonsense that you can't stand yourself anymore? You're tired of the excuses, the stories you've been telling yourself, and the patterns you keep repeating. That was me—completely fed up with where I was and how I kept getting in my own way.

I was sitting at the table, staring at my piles of bills, and I just broke down. Tears were streaming down my face because, deep down, I knew I was the one holding myself back. It wasn't just about the money or the bills—it was about the disappointment I felt in myself for staying stuck for so long. I couldn't even see the numbers on the statements through my tears. All I could see were the years of frustration and self-sabotage pouring out of me as those tears hit the paper. It was my breaking point.

As I looked out the door, watching my kids playing happily, I felt like a complete failure. How was I going to call my parents and tell them I failed and had no money to pay my bills? How was I going to tell my kids that we had to leave our home?

So, I made a decision. The word 'decide' means cutting off everything except what truly matters, and looking back, this was the most important decision I think I've ever made. I was determined to turn things around, no matter what. I knew that building a better relationship with my money was the key. It was the difference that would change everything.

I started by making some phone calls.

I called each of the companies that I owed money to, starting with the red letter ones, and for the first time, I was really honest with them about the situation I had gotten myself into. I was able to work out a repayment plan with them, so I got to keep the lights on.

I called my bank again and asked them for help. They helped me consolidate my credit cards into a personal loan, which meant the repayments weren't draining my account every week. They also helped me set up my bank accounts correctly, so I always had money for my bills.

I looked around my house for anything I could sell. I sold the cots and strollers we didn't need anymore. I sold some furniture and a lot of outfits and shoes from my wardrobe. If I didn't absolutely need it, I sold it.

My Journey of Financial Empowerment

I started paying attention to those bank statements. I pulled them out of the drawer and studied them. I learnt about my spending habits and couldn't believe how much money I had wasted over the years.

I figured out my numbers. I knew how much was coming in and, more importantly, how much was going out. I was getting into the finer details.

From that day on, I have had a monthly money date. I sit with my money, go over my numbers, look at my goals and make any necessary adjustments.

As I began to change my money situation, I also changed how I viewed it. Instead of seeing money as something to be feared or avoided, I began to see it as a tool that could support my goals and dreams. I allowed myself to appreciate and even love money—not for the sake of greed, but as a way to create opportunities and choices. This was a big shift for me. I learnt to see money as a friend rather than an adversary.

And let me tell you, once I made this shift, so much of my life changed. Suddenly, budgeting wasn't just about crunching numbers—it was about reclaiming my power, taking control of my future, and stepping into a life of abundance and wealth. I went from feeling trapped and anxious to feeling empowered and confident. I realised that having money didn't mean I was materialistic or selfish—it meant I was in control of my destiny.

Now, I'm not saying it was easy. There were bumps along the road, moments of doubt, and plenty of setbacks. But with each step forward, I felt myself growing stronger, more confident, and more aligned with my core values and desires. I felt a deep sense of relief and pride as I watched my financial situation improve. I was no longer playing games with my money, waiting on the roll of the dice to determine my future. Instead, I was navigating a steady path towards financial freedom and personal fulfilment.

I used to have a love-hate relationship with money—I loved having it and spending it, but I hated managing it. But from the moment I made that decision, sitting at my dining table, I committed to taking my money seriously. I began to nurture my finances, and since then, everything has changed.

Today, I'm incredibly proud of my financial journey. I've learnt to embrace and celebrate my achievements, no matter how small. My money has become a source of strength and empowerment, and it's allowed me to make choices that align with my true self. I feel a profound sense of freedom and joy knowing I'm living on my own terms.

That's why I'm here today, sharing this story with you. Because I want you to know that if I can do it, so can you. I'm going to share EVERYTHING I did to change my situation with money. In the chapters you're about to read, I provide you with the steps I took and the tools I used to get to where I am today. Because it worked for me, I know it can work for you.

You have the power to transform your money and break free of the beliefs and behaviours holding you back to create a life of true abundance. So, let's start this journey together. Let's rewrite your financial stories, reclaim your power, and step into abundance. Here's to your amazing transformation!

CHAPTER ONE

Set Up Your Success

You may have noticed this isn't your ordinary book about personal finances.

A lot of the books you read on money management do an introduction, then jump straight into the numbers. And that's great because we need to know how money works so that we can work it to our advantage.

But one of the things I've noticed is they lack the mindset that goes with the money. And I believe you cannot have one without the other.

In order to set you up properly and give you a red-hot crack at success, we're going to take a small but important detour and make sure that you have all the things you need to make this work. After all, if you're going to bake a cake, you need to make sure you have all the ingredients before you turn on the oven.

We're going to 'get your head in the game' by looking at conscious living, which means living on purpose and not bobbing along on the ocean relying on the tide to take you places.

We're going to look at some unique (not conventional at all) ways to cope with fear when it comes up, and it will. If you're not already feeling it, which I have a sneaking suspicion that you are, it will come up as we get into the actual money stuff. You need to know what to do so that you don't slide backwards.

We're going to learn how your mental and financial health is linked. If your finances are in a good place, you'll feel more in control, which will free up your mind and heart to focus on other things.

You're reading a book about money, so it makes sense that we're going to start talking about your money. It's about becoming comfortable with getting real about your situation and then doing something about it. If we can't have a real and frank conversation about your money, we'll never get to the heart of it and make it better.

I think it's safe to say you didn't get in the position you're in overnight. You didn't just wake up this morning and feel like money was a struggle. It's probably been like that for a while. So, we're going to talk about taking things one day at a time. Small, imperfect steps done every day will make the biggest difference to your overall results.

And finally, we're going to ditch the excuses. These are the things that have been keeping you small and stuck. You're an amazing, intelligent, resourceful woman who deserves so much happiness and joy in her life. Don't believe me? You will soon because we're going to put some things in place to help you let go of the excuses and embrace your new life.

Remember, this is your life we're talking about, and I want the absolute, undeniable, indisputable, complete and total success you rightfully deserve.

So, grab a pen and paper and let's get to work.

Live Consciously

So many of us just plod our way through life. Going where the tide takes us. No real plans. Each year is similar, if not the same, as the last. We're affected by the situations around us and are impacted by other people's needs and desires.

We've been doing this for so long that we've probably forgotten what it's like to have 'free will' and be spontaneous and a little bit selfish.

One of the most empowering benefits of taking control of your finances is the ability to live more consciously and intentionally. With this newfound clarity, you can make choices that align with your values and dreams. This is your opportunity to explore new paths, invest in your passions, and create a life that reflects your unique desires. It's time to embrace this chapter with confidence and purpose.

Living consciously means deciding for yourself what you want your life to look and feel like. Who you want to be and what you want to do and have that will fill your soul.

You don't have to compromise anymore. You don't have to put your goals and wishes aside any longer. You get to be the star of your life.

Living consciously is not only liberating but also a fundamental cornerstone of changing your financial situation because when you live consciously, you're deliberately putting the pieces of your life exactly where you want them. You're crafting your world to look and feel how you've always dreamed.

Chances are that the life you've envisioned for yourself is different from the one you're currently living. If this is you, I want you to know that it's okay to acknowledge this moment as it's a reflection of what is important—it validates your journey and the emotional weight of your experiences. And remember that this is also a time to embrace new possibilities and dreams. You have the power to redefine your future and create a life that aligns with your true self and aspirations.

To begin to live consciously, you need to be clear about what your dream lifestyle looks like and what it feels like to live it. Then, we'll know what your bank accounts and your money situation need to look like to make it happen.

In your notepad, take as much time as you need to answer these questions.

Don't rush this part because this is where we'll paint the picture of the incredible lifestyle you want to live now.

Be wild. Be bold. Be crazy when you think about these questions. Allow yourself to indulge in some fantasies and be in a place where everything is possible.

If there were no limitations in your life…

- What would you feel as a successful woman?
- What would you think?
- What would you believe?

- How would you behave?
- What worries, stressors or fears would you let go of?
- How would you conduct yourself when it comes to your money? Spending? Saving? Shopping?
- What would enjoying your life and your money feel like?
- What is your self-trust like?
- What would stepping into the full version of a successful woman be like for you?
- What would becoming this woman do for you?
    - What do you know?
    - How do you feel?
    - What inspires you?
    - What brings you happiness and joy?
    - What motivates you?
    - How do you take action?
    - What actions would you likely take?

Important:

When you're writing the answers to these questions, make sure that you write them in a positive way.

For example, "I don't want to be afraid anymore," becomes "I am a fearless woman." Or, "I don't want to struggle with money," becomes "I am money savvy and live an abundant life."

Once you have answered these questions, I want you to read the answers aloud to yourself every morning before you get out of bed. Set the alarm for 10 minutes earlier than normal. Take five deep breaths and read your answers aloud to yourself.

At first, you might feel a little silly, but that will pass, and you'll begin to absorb the feelings and start becoming the woman in your dreams.

Practise feeling and thinking in line with your answers. Feel and think as though you're her and you have what she has, and the possibilities and opportunities are already yours.

I have a little notebook that sits on my bedside table. It's filled with answers to questions just like these in almost every area of my life. I have deliberately decided how I want my life to be. No compromise. No excuses. No settling. I am the conscious creator of my life, and every day, I choose an area to focus on, read that section, and breathe life into my dreams.

I'm becoming the woman in my little notebook. And she is absolutely, incredibly, wholeheartedly amazing.

Fear

One of the biggest challenges I had to confront during this change in my life was the fear of getting it wrong and making my bad situation even worse. It wasn't just the fear of messing up once—it was the worry that every mistake could send me spiralling into an even deeper financial hole.

I had these runaway thoughts that went something like this...

I make a wrong financial move, can't pay my bills, lose everything, and end up in a situation I can't recover from.

Or...

I try to fix my money problems, but instead of getting better, they get worse, and I'm left even more stuck than before.

And even this one...

I make a poor decision with my money, and it ruins any chance I have of turning my life around.

These thoughts hit like lightning and then stick around, sometimes for days or even months, playing on a loop in the background of my mind. They always seem to end up with some worst-case scenario, like I've catastrophised my way into the most impossible situation.

I won't lie—those fears are still there. They're just not as loud as they used to be. I'm not sure they'll ever completely disappear, but I've learnt how to manage them now.

It's Dr. John Demartini who says that fear is simply an acronym— **Future Expectations Appearing Real**. He says it's the projection that, in the future, you'll experience more pain than pleasure, more hurt than joy, more sadness than happiness, more failure than success. And for me, this rings true to the core of my being.

> **If you want to explore more of Dr. John Demartini's teachings, I recommend you start with The Breakthrough Experience. I have spent many hours devouring his work and attending his seminars to learn from him personally, and it has helped me change my life.*

Fear is a necessary part of the human experience. It has been built into us on purpose to keep us safe when there's a perceived threat to our existence, which is why we often feel like we're going to die when we get scared.

Fear starts in our brain and spreads throughout our whole body so we can be prepared for the best defence—fight, flight, or freeze.

The fear response starts in a region of the brain called the amygdala. It's an almond-shaped part of the brain that lives in the temporal lobe, right in the dark parts of the brain. Its whole purpose, its reason for being here, is to detect a threat to our safety and wellbeing.

This makes sense when we're walking down the road, and a big dog starts barking from behind the fence. We're often startled and instinctually jump away from the fence. Sometimes, you can find yourself running away (flight response). Other times, you yell back at the dog and tell it to 'settle down' (fight response). There are also times when you can find yourself just standing there, unsure of what to do, looking around to see if anyone else is there who can help you (freeze response).

After a split second of assessing the situation, we consciously know that we're going to be okay. The dog is behind the fence. The fence is strong and will keep the dog away. There's no real threat. We re-label the experience (stoopid dog!) and carry on as we were before. We're now at a place where we feel in control again.

The perception of control is so important to how we experience and respond to fear.

When we overcome the initial fight, flight, or freeze response, we feel satisfied, reassured of our safety and more confident that we can do this.

But what happens when our fear is of something that hasn't happened yet? What happens if we're afraid of something that may or may not happen in the future? I mean, you can walk (or run) away from a dog, but what do you do when the fear is imagined?

Set Up Your Success

I like to think of fear as a little soldier that lives in my unconscious mind. He looks a little medieval and has a full suit of armour on. He has a sword in one hand and a shield in the other. He patrols the boundaries of my mind 24/7/365. He never takes a day off. When I'm asleep, he's on hyper-alert, always making sure that I'm safe and secure (bless him...😊).

The problem is that he has a direct line to my thoughts and can't determine if they're real or imagined. He sees everything as real.

So, when he hears my thoughts about my fears, he goes to DEFCOM 10 and prepares for battle.

The good news is that he's doing exactly what he's supposed to do. His job is to keep me safe, and if he gets even the slightest whiff that something is a threat, he's onto it (again, bless him...).

He would love it if I stayed inside, locked all the doors and windows, pulled all the curtains and blinds closed and never answered the phone. Then he would know I was safe and secure.

But let's be honest, who wants to live like that?

Because he can hear my thoughts, I like to write to him. I thank him for all the good work he's doing to keep me safe and secure. Then, I tell him how sad I'm feeling because of the fear I'm experiencing. I tell him that I don't want to feel scared and sad anymore. I explain to him what I want to do and how I want to feel.

Now, this little guy only wants me to be happy. And somehow, when he hears my thoughts and I put them in writing, DEFCOM 10 becomes smaller and quieter, and the churning in my chest and my racing thoughts all seem to calm down.

That works well for a perceived fear, but what happens when the fear is real?

When this happens to me (and it still does today because I'm a real person), I assess this fear by asking myself the following questions:

- Is this situation putting me at risk?
- Is this situation putting me in harm's way?
- Can I do something about it?

If it's a yes to any of these questions, then I need a plan to mitigate the risk and harm.

If it's a financial risk, like I've received a big bill I'm not sure how I'm going to pay, and it's keeping me awake at night and giving me anxiety, I need to do something about it.

So, here's what I do:

- I take the fear out of the shadows.
    - For example, if it's a big electricity bill, my fear is that I won't be able to afford to pay it, my electricity will be turned off, and I will freeze to death because it's winter.
- I assess the risk.
    - Does this risk impact my health and well-being? Yes, I don't want to freeze to death.
- I look for potential solutions.
    - How many paydays until the bill is due? Two
    - Am I able to average the bill out over the next few pay periods until it's due? Yes
    - Am I able to get an extension on my bill? Yes
    - Am I able to borrow some money from someone? No

- Am I able to sell anything to pay the bill? Possibly
      - Am I able to get any overtime or work an extra shift? Yes
- I take action.
      - I call the electricity company and get an extension on my due date.
      - I make a partial payment every payday until the full amount is paid

The risk is being managed. I have a plan that the electricity company has agreed on. I just need to execute the plan.

Here's another example…

I changed jobs a few years ago and went from monthly pay to fortnightly pay. Now, I love monthly pay. I get to manage my money once a month and don't have to worry about it until the next month. I had organised for all my outgoing expenses to come out of my accounts the day after my monthly pay. So, on the 16th of each month, all my payments would come out of the bank, and everything would be paid on time.

Now, going from monthly pay to fortnightly pay is challenging. I was used to getting a full month's pay. So, that first fortnightly pay had to pay all my monthly bills. It was a little tight, to say the least.

Needless to say, I wasn't going to be able to make all my payments. So, here's what I did:

- I took the fear out of the shadows—I was afraid that I wouldn't be able to pay all my bills on time.
- I looked at it as clinically as I possibly could—there were more bills than money.
- I assessed the risk—I was at risk of overdrawing my account and defaulting on my bills, which would incur

overdraw fees from my bank and may impact my credit history.
- I looked for potential solutions—can I defer any bills? Could I get any extensions? Could I take any money out of my savings? Or, in the worst-case scenario, could I borrow money from anyone? (It's not my favourite, but sometimes you have to ask for help.)
- I took action—I emailed my property manager and explained the situation. I asked her if it was okay to pay my rent a few days late, and because I had always paid my rent early, she was happy to help me. I emailed the provider of a course I was doing, explained the situation, and asked if we could move my direct debit date to the end of the month instead of the middle. Because I had always made my payments on time, they were happy to help me. I also called my electricity company and asked for an extension on my next bill. Again, because of my good payment history, I was able to get that extension.

Crisis averted! I was able to rearrange my finances, pay all my bills across the month and not dip into my long-term savings.

It took probably two hours to get all that done, and by the time it was all sorted, I had an action plan that was workable, and my fear was gone.

Fear is one of those things that can keep you paralysed and stuck. But once you take it out of the dark and look at it with a logical lens, its potency begins to dilute, and you take back control of your situation. A win-win all around.

Set Up Your Success

Financial Health and Mental Health are Linked

Have you ever spent a sleepless night tossing and turning, stressing about how you're going to pay your bills? I know I have. More times than I care to admit.

It's one of those things that can be really isolating. You don't want to call anyone at 2 am and say, "Hey, I've run out of money, and I don't know what I'm going to do. Got a minute??"

I remember back when I started using the steps in this book, I started to see my debts reduce and my savings increase. It was like the seesaw was finally tipping in the right direction.

I would see a pair of shoes or an outfit, and I would know that there was money in my 'splurge fund' to buy it. Or I wouldn't feel like cooking, so I would take myself out to dinner and enjoy a really nice meal cooked by someone else. Bliss!

I remember the feeling of going to the checkout with a trolley full of groceries and not batting an eyelid because there was plenty of money to cover it. Whatever the cost.

This was such a stark contrast to the earlier days. Shopping was a nightmare. I would mentally calculate each item that went into the trolley so that I didn't blow my weekly grocery budget. I wouldn't look at clothes or shoes because it would make me feel dreadful. Paying the bills and making ends meet was stressful and an exercise in robbing Peter to pay Paul.

The difference in how I felt about myself, my situation, and the world during each of these times of my life is so incredible. When there was money in the bank, I felt amazing. Carefree. On top of the world. When money was really tight, I felt stressed. Anxious. Cautious. And definitely highly strung.

There's a definitive link between our financial health and our mental health. I'd even include our emotional health here as well.

A certain relaxedness comes about when we have our money in order. A peace of mind that permeates itself around our whole world.

The feelings of freedom, self-assuredness and light-heartedness take over and allow us to focus our attention on other areas of our lives.

So, this book has come about at a really good time for you. As you read and work your way through the chapters, don't be surprised that you'll feel a little lighter and a little brighter as your financial house gets into order. Over time, it becomes addictive, and you'll wonder how you ever did things before.

Talking Money

When I was a kid, there were a few rules in our household:

1. Children should be seen and not heard
2. We don't talk after dinner (that's TV time)
3. We don't discuss politics, religion, or money

So, I grew up never having discussed money. I knew that my dad went to work and brought home the bacon, and my mum was a stay-at-home mum. Dad would give her his pay, and she would miraculously turn that into the nice life we led.

My brother and I both went to private schools. We got a good education. We had holidays. We lived in a big two-storey house. We wanted for nothing.

Set Up Your Success

But how did she do all that on one income? To this day, I have no idea.

Money talk was one of those things that just wasn't done in my household. It was one of the most private things that was never discussed.

As a consequence, I never learnt how to manage money.

I used to see money as something to be spent. If I had $20 left in my bank account, that was $20 I could spend on something (usually some junk that would break or fall apart in the next 48 hours).

Retirement...that's for old people.

Buying a house...maybe someday.

I spent the first few years of my marriage either broke or close to broke. We were both bad with money, and to make matters worse, we each thought we could do it better than the other.

Consequently, at the end of my marriage, when our house was sold and everything was divided up and squared away, we were still in debt. Not huge amounts, but enough to make you wonder where all the money went in the 13 years that we were together. We had nothing to show for our efforts except an ugly debt and an intense dislike for each other. It kind of rubbed salt into the wound for me.

I believe **now** is the best time to take money out of the shadows and start to talk about it. And I mean really talk about it.

The fastest-growing demographic of homeless people is women over 50. And that scares the pants off me.

A lot of us have been stay-at-home mums (I was for many years), our husbands have handled the money side of things, and we haven't had the same income because we worked part-time; therefore, our superannuation or retirement funds aren't as high as our husbands' or partners.

We often leave our marriage but stay in our homes because of the emotional connection. However, this can leave us in a worse position because it used to take two incomes to run the house, and now you're down to working four days a week and stressing at 2 am because the oven stopped working and you have no idea how you're going to pay to get it fixed.

I'm feeling stressed just thinking about it.

So, now is a good time to start talking money. Turn on the light, take it out of the shadows, and have a real, hearty conversation about how we're going to live our lives. How we're going to go from being stressed at checkout to I'll have those shoes in black *and* tan, thanks. Imagine that!!

By having this conversation throughout this book, we're going to put you back in the pilot seat so you'll have the ultimate control over your future. So exciting!!

No More Excuses

One of the things we really need to do when we're creating a new chapter in our lives is to let go of our excuses. They're not serving you at all. If anything, they're keeping you small and stuck. And that's definitely not what I want for you.

As human beings, we're wired to 'justify' why things are or aren't the way they appear.

Set Up Your Success

I'm too old

I'm not smart enough

I'm divorced

My ex is a d@$%head*

I didn't get the house

I got the house

I have too much debt

I don't make enough money

I'm not good with money

I can't do maths

I don't know where to start

You name it, I've heard it all. And some that would even curl your ears…

You'll never progress or move forward out of this space you're currently in if you continue to make excuses. So, let's put a little light on those excuses and give them a bit of an antidote:

> *I'm too old*—Vera Wang became a famous fashion designer after the age of 40, and she didn't open her first bridal boutique until she was 50.
>
> *I'm not smart enough*—adult education is a booming industry, particularly online learning.

Saving Myself

I'm divorced—yes, you are and with that comes a whole lot of new opportunities you didn't have before.

My ex is a d@$%head*—whose isn't? That's why they're your ex, remember?

I didn't get the house—you get to have a complete do-over.

I got the house—you get to keep your memories.

I have too much debt—I have a few tips that can help you fix that.

I don't make enough money—side hustle anyone?

I'm not good with money—that's why I'm here and you're reading this book.

I can't do maths—there's a calculator on your smartphone.

I don't know where to start—good thing you've got this book!

You get to choose whether you want to stay small and stuck in excuses or be free to live your life. The choice is completely yours. There's no right or wrong choice here. It's what's best for you. Just keep in mind that each choice will take you down a different path.

When you hear yourself making an excuse, stop yourself mid-sentence and replace it with something more empowering.

Instead of, "I can't do this," say, "Of course, I can do this."

Instead of, "This is too hard," say, "I'm learning something new every day."

> Instead of saying, "I'm not good with money," say, "Money and I have a great relationship that is growing daily."

It will take some effort on your part and a certain amount of willpower to stop making excuses, but it's not impossible. You're developing new positive money habits that will support your dreams and goals. We will go into all things habits later in the book.

Let today be the day that you stop with the excuses and start making plans.

One Day at a Time

One of the most important things to remember with all of this is that it's going to take time. This book, my methodologies, advice (non-financial, of course), and ideas will all take time to come about.

There's no silver bullet when it comes to rebuilding your finances. Everyone's journey is different. And it's important to remember that you come with your own set of dreams and limitations on what you can and cannot do.

So, my advice to you on this one is to take things one day at a time. Be enthusiastic, but don't be in a frantic rush. Be excited, but don't push yourself too hard. Take small, imperfect steps, like the ones in this book, and you'll begin to turn the corner and move away from the anxiety that accompanies you when you're trying to manage your money. You'll begin to see life through a new lens. A new way of living. And you're going to love it. I know I do.

It's Your Turn

Now, it's your turn to start making a new life for yourself.

> *I always picture a phoenix rising from the ashes when I think of my life now. Somehow, it always pops into my head—Harry Potter style!*

Here's a list of things that we covered in this chapter that'll help you set yourself up for success:

- ☐ Make a decision right now to begin to live consciously and commit to it
- ☐ Write a letter to your fear and ask it for help
- ☐ Put your financial, mental, and emotional health at the top of your priority list
- ☐ Start to be more open about your money to gain clarity
- ☐ Catch yourself when you start to make excuses and replace them with something more empowering
- ☐ Commit to making one small, imperfect step every day

Remember, you're not alone. I'll be with you every step of the way. We'll do this together. And together, we'll kick off your next and best chapter yet. Let's do it!!

CHAPTER TWO

Begin Your Business

Why is it that we seem to have a different mindset at work than we do at home? We show up to work on time each and every day. We work hard and get results. When we have our annual performance review, we take pride in obtaining great scores, which boosts our confidence and commitment.

So why is it that the attitude and approach we have towards work can be different than the one we have towards our personal lives?

For many of us, managing our personal finances can feel daunting. However, it doesn't have to, especially if we apply how we manage our work to our personal finances.

Building and managing a business requires structure. It takes planning, process and systems to make it work.

So, what can we learn from running a business, and how can we apply that knowledge to our personal finances?

You Inc.

One of the biggest changes I made to my financial situation was to start seeing my money as a business.

You Inc. (or Jo Inc. in my case) is how I design my life. I treat it like a business. (Stay with me here, you'll understand in a minute.)

Jo Inc. has money coming in (revenue—my salary), money going out (expenses—my bills) and money left over (reserves—my savings).

I've regained the ultimate control and perspective by seeing my life as a business.

Here are the key components of You Inc.:

- The chief executive officer (CEO) leads the way and gets to decide where you're going and what you're going to be doing.
- The chief operating officer (COO) manages the operations and is the engine behind You Inc.
- The chief financial officer (CFO) provides the funding and the budgets to ensure that You Inc. gets to where it wants to go.

Depending on the type of life you want to create for yourself, you can have many more roles in your life's business, like treasurer, marketing officer, receptionist, caterer, or engineer. It's totally up to you what roles you have and how you set up your life's business.

Begin Your Business

Now, here's the kicker...

Each time I need to make a decision (a significant decision, not what I'm going to wear that day…well, not unless you have a fashion designer in your business), I assume the role that's responsible for that area of my life.

For example, suppose I need to make a decision about replacing my fridge. In that case, I become the CFO, review the financial status of Jo Inc., and determine whether or not there's enough funding for this project and if there will be a return on my investment.

If I need to make a decision on where I'm going to live, I need to view it through the lens of the CEO. I ask myself if this decision is going to keep me and Jo Inc. on the path to achieving our purpose. If it does, then I can progress to the next stage. If it doesn't, I can find another option.

By assuming the position relevant to the choice I need to make, I take a lot of emotion out of the decision-making process, just like we do at work, and I can choose what's in my overall best interests.

Now, I'm not saying that my life is all work and no play because it isn't. I have my Friday night drinks. I have an amazing Christmas party. I celebrate my successes and I lick my wounds when it all goes pear-shaped.

And, of course, there are times when those shoes just call my name, and I buy them regardless of what the CFO might say. But hey, I'm only human and, let's face it, they're shoes!! A girl's gotta live.

Your Mission Statement

If you look at any business, whether it's a big conglomerate or a small business in your local area, you'll most likely find that they have a mission statement.

While many of them are bland and not really specific, there's a reason why nearly every business has one.

Mission statements help businesses stay aligned with the values they find most important and ensure they're staying focused on the way they want to impact the world.

So, if mission statements are so crucial that businesses often spend hundreds of hours and a lot of money fine-tuning them, why do so few people take the time to create their own personal mission statement?

A personal mission statement is the number one tool for making tough decisions. It helps to create boundaries that allow you to play, create, and live freely.

Everything, from your investments of time, money and relationships, should fit within the boundaries of your mission statement.

Boundaries aren't necessarily the first thing that comes to mind when you think about freedom, but they're essential to avoid distractions and free yourself up to focus on the things you find most important.

Once you have set the boundaries for what you will and won't accept in your life, when something comes up that's outside those boundaries, you don't even have a decision to make. It's that simple.

Once you declare your mission statement, you begin living it. You don't have to consider much outside of it. The statement can be as long or as short as you like.

Here's mine for myself and my business:

> *My mission is to help others restore calm, change their habits and live their life from the heart.*

I have spent a great amount of time thinking about my mission statement. It has gone through multiple iterations and changes as I have grown and changed myself.

You can't just pull a meaningful personal mission statement out of thin air. But with the right questions and a bit of time and effort, you can create one that has you sitting up and taking notice.

There are questions you can begin asking yourself every day that will help you create your own personal mission statement:

1. What is important? What/whom do I value? How is my life connected to those things?
2. Where do I want to go? You can answer this in many different ways. Your answer may involve a spiritual, mental, or physical destination. It might describe your career.
3. What does "the best" look like for me? Describe your best possible result. This isn't the time to be realistic. This is the time to dream.
4. How do I want to act? How do I want people to describe me? Think of a few words you would want to come to mind when people think about you.
5. What kind of legacy do I want to leave behind? Imagine you're 100 years in the future. What does the impact you've left look like? How is your Butterfly Effect still touching lives?

Write down the answers to these questions and revisit them as often as you need to. As you continue thinking about them, begin giving your personal mission statement a go.

Here are a few hints:

Keep it short. You want this to be something you can sum up in a single sentence. Remember, this is about focusing your life on what matters most.

Don't forget about others. Yes, this is a personal mission statement, but it should be just as much about the people you want to impact as it is about yourself.

Share it with the most important people in your life. Get feedback from them. They can provide you with invaluable insights.

It's ok to make changes. As you grow and continue learning, your mission might evolve (just like mine has). That's natural and quite normal. As long as you're staying true to the mission you know you were put here to accomplish, you can't go wrong.

Important note:

If you find that you're overwhelmed when you're thinking about your personal mission statement and feel that you're not sure about what you want to do tomorrow, let alone with the rest of your life, it's ok to shorten the timeframe quite significantly.

You can choose for your life's purpose to be relevant for the next year if you want to. If that feels too big, make it for the next three months or seven days. Your personal mission statement could be as simple as:

> *To become the person I need to be to create the quality of life that I truly want.*

Or...

> *I'm going to smile more so that I can bring a little more happiness to my life and those around me.*

Living every day in alignment with your personal mission statement, constantly and consciously aligning your thoughts, words and actions, inspires you to wake up every day and make better choices that enable you to live in alignment with your purpose.

Rearview Mirror

I remember the first time my dad took me out for a driving lesson. He's an engineer, so everything is precise and to the point.

We were down the road from home at a new housing estate. The roads had just been laid with bitumen, and the markers were on the blocks to signify the boundaries of the new properties.

I remember sitting there and wondering how on earth I was going to do this. I was taught to drive in a manual car. There were three pedals, but I only had two feet. I had to look out the windscreen so that I could see where I was going. I had to check my side mirrors so that I could see what was happening beside me. And I had to watch my rearview mirror to see what was going on behind me.

Saving Myself

Three pedals—two feet

Three mirrors—but keep your eyes on the road

One gear stick—but keep both hands on the steering wheel

Seriously...how on earth was I going to learn how to do this?

It took me years to get my license. I just wasn't any good at driving. The maths alone didn't work for me and I would make myself dizzy all the time. I'd be looking out at the road ahead, looking at the side mirrors, looking in the rearview mirror and repeating the process over and over so many times that I ended up with a head spin and had to pull over. My dad would look at me as if I was ready for the lunatic asylum. Happy days!

Looking back, I can see that I was just overcomplicating something that now is so simple. In fact, I can get from my home to the shops and back again without raising a sweat. I can do it without even thinking. Hell, I can do it while belting out *Drops of Jupiter* as if Train was watching *me* with awe.

I can do this now because, during one driving lesson, my dad told me to pull over. I was on the verge of tears, thinking, 'I'm never going to get this...can someone call me a taxi, please?'

Dad told me that I didn't have to look in all the mirrors all the time. They were there just for quick glances and to adjust what I saw. If I could see a car in my rearview mirror and they were too close, I could merge into another lane and let them pass.

That advice has stayed with me since.

The rearview mirror, the one that lets you see behind you, is only necessary for quick glances and to make adjustments.

So, as you begin this new chapter of your life and build your new personal business, use your rearview mirror scarcely. Because, while you're constantly looking behind you, you'll miss out on what's in front of you. And what's in front of you is You Inc.

Draw a Line in the Sand

Your whole life changes the day you make the decision to draw a line in the sand and commit to doing things differently.

When you realise that this minute in time is that pivotal moment that could change your life, things start to change.

Or, of course, you can choose to be the same as you've always been. To continue with life the way it is. To stay stuck and in pain while you watch everyone else get on with it. It's your right to decide. I won't judge you, I promise.

Some people aren't ready to change. They're not ready to let go of their past hurt. They're literally stuck, and if that's you, I wish you all the love in the world and hope that this will shift for you one day.

But if you're ready to let go, turn your life around, and become the CEO of You Inc., draw a line in the sand and make today the day that you choose you.

It's Your Turn

Seeing your life as part business and part personal creates an interesting dynamic. It allows you to have the structure (business) you need and enjoy (personal) the fruits of your labour.

Here are the steps to complete for this chapter:

- ☐ Name your business (mine is 'Jo Inc.') and decide on the roles you'll fill.
- ☐ Write your personal mission statement.
- ☐ Commit to small, short glances in the rearview mirror and don't spend your time focused on the past.
- ☐ Draw a line in the sand that says, "Today, I choose me."

CHAPTER THREE

Shift Your Story

From our earliest moments in life, we've been told stories. Our parents told us stories. Our teachers told us stories. Our grandparents. Aunts. Uncles. Friends. You name it. From the beginning of our lives, we've been told stories.

Storytelling began with visual stories, like cave drawings, and gradually shifted to word of mouth. Then, they changed into tales and were performed in dances or plays. These tales were then written down into books, which have even shifted to the digital format we see today.

Storytelling is as old as time. For a lot of cultures across the world, stories were how they entertained each other, passed down traditions and taught lessons to generation after generation.

Stories are how we make sense of our world. Through the stories we're told, we can inherit the attitudes and values of our families. This can affect our emotional connection to money and, therefore, how we end up managing it.

Growing up, how were finances handled in your family? Were the financial expectations different for your father than for your mother? Who had the most influence on your money story?

What we were taught about money from our family directly affects our financial beliefs. Did your family believe that money was good or bad? Did they see it as a necessary evil? Was it there to be spent or saved? Is it hard to obtain or easy to get your hands on?

Your family's money story has a flow-on effect on how you perceive money today. When you look at your current situation, are you happy with it? Do you know how much money and assets you have? Do you know how much debt you have? Are you happy with the amount of money you're earning and where it goes?

How do you feel about your money? Do you feel empowered to make financial decisions? Do you still feel like you have to ask permission to spend money, even though you're living on your own now?

When you ask yourself these questions, you're opening up your mind to your money story. You get insight into how and why you manage your money the way that you do.

You'll also find it easier to start talking about money when you have a better understanding of your own money story and the emotional connection you have to it.

Your Money Story

Your money story has developed over time but originally started with your parents. You begin handling money the way that they did. Then, you add your own personal style to the mix.

Have you always wanted things now, or are you patient and know that small steps will often help you achieve your goals? Do you live in the moment, or is your head in the clouds dreaming of a better life? Are you a spender or a saver? Do you live in the moment or have long-term goals?

Your money story and the way you think about saving, budgeting, and spending influence your behaviour and financial situation.

If you want to change your money story and bring about more stability and security in your financial house, you must first identify how you may be derailing your finances and reflect on how you can create a new money story that will support you and You Inc.

A positive money story built on the belief that you're good with money, know how to save, and will always be taken care of can help you grow your finances exponentially. Whereas a negative money story that focuses on scarcity and lack, believing that you'll never get out of debt or that money is hard to come by can hold you back and prevent you from achieving financial success.

As your money story shapes your financial reality, knowing if it empowers or disempowers you is crucial.

The first step to updating your money story is to begin writing down everything you tell yourself about money. For example:

I'm a spender, not a saver

I'm not good with money

I'll never be able to get out of debt

I'll never be able to afford to buy a home of my own

There's never enough money to pay my bills

As soon as I get some savings, a bill always comes in, and I end up with nothing again

By writing these down, you'll uncover the limiting beliefs that are unconsciously driving your behaviours and are holding you back from achieving financial success.

When you see them written down in front of you, you'll understand why you're not getting ahead financially. You'll also begin taking control of your spending and saving habits.

Forgiveness

If you don't like what you see once you have uncovered your current money story, this is a great moment in your life!

You now have the opportunity to rewrite your money story to one that will empower you and help you create a life of prosperity and abundance.

Now, the last thing you want to do right now is give yourself a hard time because your money story isn't empowering you. This isn't the time to be adding more guilt and baggage (and more negative stories) into your life.

Shift Your Story

So, I want you to forgive yourself for your past money story. I know for a fact that if you could have done it better, you would have.

You've just become aware of something that's not serving you and are about to learn something new. It's time to be kind and gentle and forgive yourself for not knowing a better way.

Choose a New Story

While money beliefs can be passed on from one generation to another, they don't have to be permanent. Now that you realise that your old money story isn't serving you anymore, it's time to create a new, positive money story.

Make a list of ten positive money beliefs that will serve you and help you create a life of abundance and prosperity. Here's a list to help you get started:

   I create my life

   I'm committed to my own abundance and prosperity

   I'm excellent at receiving wealth into my life

   Money brings calmness and spare time

   I'm very good with money

   Money can buy lots of great time with my loved ones

   I'm a money magnet

   I'm comfortable asking for help with money

Saving Myself

I'm learning about money every day

I love money, and money loves me

I'm aware of every cent that comes out of my pocket

I always have money

Money is a magnifier

I'm happy with what I have, and I want more

I can be wealthy and modest

I can learn anything I need about money

Having money is easy

I accept the abundance in life with gratitude

Using money brings me joy and happiness

It feels great to have money

I'm so proud of myself for being prosperous

I give myself permission to buy things that make me happy

Money in the bank is hot!

Once you have your list, type it, print it, and stick it on a wall, on your fridge, or in your bedroom so that it's the first thing you see when you wake up in the morning.

Shift Your Story

Repeating these money beliefs as often as you can will create new neural pathways in your brain, creating a new way of thinking.

Each time you catch yourself repeating your old money story, stop yourself mid-sentence (even mid-word) and replace it with your new money story.

This will take a bit of time and practice, but each time you repeat your new money story, you're cementing the new neural pathway and building a stronger money story.

It's Your Turn

Now, it's your turn to create a new, positive money story that will support you as you rebuild your finances:

- ☐ Begin writing down everything you tell yourself about money.
- ☐ Forgive yourself for your past money story (this could be as simple as writing yourself a letter).
- ☐ Make a list of 10 positive money beliefs that will serve you and help you create a life of abundance and prosperity.
- ☐ Print out or write down your new positive money story and stick it around your house as a reminder of the abundance and prosperity you're creating.

CHAPTER FOUR

Manage Your Mindset

Have you ever heard the saying, "What you think about, you bring about"? It's basically saying what you think, you become.

Your mindset directly affects how you see the world. If you have a 'glass half empty' mindset, you'll consistently see the world as lacking. You'll often attribute any failures or stumbling blocks directly to your lack of skill or ability. If you have a 'glass half full' mindset, your world will be filled with abundance and opportunity. You think that good things will happen, so they will.

Your mindset is how you make sense of the world around you. It influences how you think, feel and act in any given situation.

It's rooted in your experiences, education and culture, and from there, you've established your thoughts, beliefs and attitudes. Those thoughts, beliefs, and attitudes lead to certain actions, and with those actions, you have your own experiences.

A strong and positive mindset is essential to developing healthy self-esteem. It's an important tool that affects your daily self-talk and reinforces your most intimate beliefs, attitudes, and feelings about yourself. And it's particularly important when it comes to your money.

Fixed Mindset

There are two types of mindsets—the fixed mindset and the growth mindset.

A fixed mindset is a belief that our qualities are fixed traits that we cannot change. People with this mindset believe that talent alone leads to success.

People with a fixed mindset see what happens to them as a direct measure of their competence and worth. They believe, through their own experiences as well as internal and external feedback, that this is their lot in life, and they have to play the hand they were dealt. They tell themselves things like:

    I'm a failure

    I can't do this

    I'm not smart enough

    It's too late for me

Interestingly, when they aren't facing a potential failure, they feel just as worthy and optimistic as anyone else. But when the chips are down, and something has happened to them, people with a fixed mindset have a feeling of absolute failure and paralysis.

Growth Mindset

A growth mindset is thinking that our intelligence can grow with time and experience. This mindset encourages us to put in extra time, and that effort leads to higher achievement.

People with a growth mindset see what happens to them but don't label themselves or throw their hands in the air and confess, 'It is what it is.' Even if they feel distressed, they're ready to take on the challenge and keep working at it. They believe things like:

> I'm able to learn and grow
>
> I've time to make this better
>
> I'll find someone to talk to for advice

When people with a growth mindset are facing a challenge, they see it as a learning opportunity. They recognise that they might not have the right skills or ability to tackle the challenge, so they educate themselves and get the right advice. They're open to improving their situation.

Money Mindset

If we were to chunk this down a level or two and focus specifically on your mindset when it comes to money, you'd discover whether you're someone who is successful with money or someone who just wants to give up and do it another day.

What you believe about money, yourself and the world shapes your life. Every single day, you're making decisions (consciously or unconsciously) that will move you forward financially or set you back.

Your money mindset is your unique set of beliefs and attitudes about you and how you handle money. It's the driver behind the decisions you make about saving, spending, and managing your money.

People who have a **fixed money mindset** believe things like:

> There's nothing I can do about my financial situation
>
> I have to make the best of my money situation because it will never improve

People who have a **growth money mindset** believe things like:

> I can learn how to manage my money better
>
> I can make better financial choices every day
>
> It's possible to achieve my financial goals

Your money mindset shapes how you feel about debt, your attitude toward people who make more or less than you, how easily you can pivot, and your ability to invest confidently.

It was Henry Ford who said, "Whether you believe that you can do a thing or not, you're right." What he was saying is that what you believe will drive your behaviour, which will lead to your results—either negative or positive.

Just like your money story, which we looked at earlier, your money mindset is rooted in your childhood experiences and how your family managed their money. If you heard your parents say,

Manage Your Mindset

"Money doesn't grow on trees," or overheard them discussing their tight budget and struggling to make ends meet, saying, "There's just not enough for everything," or, "We can't afford it this month," the seed of your money mindset is planted, and that seed begins to grow.

It's watered and fertilised over time by your actions and beliefs around money. If you feed it negative beliefs, it will end up being thin, brittle and have little foliage. If you feed it positive beliefs, it will flourish with big, strong branches and bright green leaves.

Years ago, I attended a seminar on public speaking and how you can monetise it. I remember talking to the speaker during a break about the amount of money she said you could make and how it was equivalent to how much service you could provide to the greater world. I was riveted by this conversation as I was during the whole seminar.

I remember saying to her, "What do you do with all that money?" She looked at me blankly. I don't think she understood my question. So I clarified and said, "When you've paid all your bills and have money left over (I mean, did that actually happen to people?), what do you do with it?" I literally couldn't wrap my head around what to do with leftover money. It was a concept that was completely foreign to me.

Her answer was to get a good financial planner and grow your money. Good advice, for sure.

But I was still stuck on the concept of 'spare money.' Who on earth was rich enough to have spare money? I grappled with it for some time (way too long, if I'm honest).

Until one day, when I decided that I was going to have some spare money, too. I mean, if they could do it, then so could I.

Saving Myself

I bought myself a little purse from the $2 shop and tucked it into one of the drawers of my bedside table. Each payday, I would take out $50 from my bank and tuck it into that little purse. I now had spare money, too! I did this payday after payday until I had $1000 in that little purse.

I felt like a superstar. I felt rich because I had spare money, which I didn't even know existed before.

I always believed that money was there to pay the bills. That was its job. If I could get all the bills paid and have some money left over for a luxury or two (usually in the form of chocolate or takeaway one night), I was winning at life. I used to look at my bank account and see my balance as 'money I had left to spend.' Savings never came into it.

The real test came when I realised I had $1000 in that little purse. My urge to spend that money was insanely strong. I could think of 10 things I could buy just off the top of my head.

I have to confess that I did spend it. On what, you ask? No idea. I cannot remember. So, it wasn't something substantial or life-changing.

I remember feeling so remorseful and upset with myself after my big spend. I had worked so hard to put that money in the little purse. I had $1000 in it. More money than I ever had. And I blew it all.

The guilt and remorse were so terrible. I had failed.

So, after shedding quite a few tears and beating myself up, I decided that I had no choice but to start again. This time, I would do things a little bit differently. I knew that once I became aware of how much money I had saved, I would be tempted to spend

Manage Your Mindset

it again. So this time, I decided that I wouldn't count the money. Then I wouldn't know how much was there and I wouldn't be tempted to spend it. I would just leave it in the little purse and keep adding to it each payday.

This time, it worked. I got used to having spare money. I got comfortable knowing there were savings there if I really needed them.

But the strangest thing happened. The fatter the little purse became, the more I wanted to add to it. And I've found that to be true even now. The more money I have in savings, tucked away for a rainy day or my big goals, the less I want to spend and the more excited I am about putting more money away.

That little purse has helped me change my whole life because now I know:

    I'm good with money

    I can save and grow my money

    I can say yes when I want to and no when I need to

    Money and I are great friends who look after each other all the time

I had gone from someone who didn't even know that spare money existed to someone who had three accounts with spare money. It all happened when my eyes were opened to a new way of living, and I changed my mind about how I wanted to live my life.

Catch Yourself

There's a saying that goes like this…"You don't know what you don't know." And I believe that to be so true.

Years ago, I didn't know that spare money was a thing. But now I know (plus a whole lot more).

I had to be really vigilant with myself when it came to saving my money. And this literally came down to my thoughts and catching myself when I started to think with a fixed money mindset.

The best way to find out whether you have a fixed money mindset or a growth money mindset is to become really conscious of your thoughts when you're paying your bills.

If you find that you're happy paying them and there's enough money left over, which gives you a good feeling and you give yourself a bit of a pat on the back, chances are you have a growth money mindset. You know there's plenty to go around, and your share comes to you easily and effortlessly.

If you find that you have to drag yourself, practically kicking and screaming, to pay your bills and the whole time you're grumpy because you'd rather be buying shoes or going out for a latte, it's safe to say you have a fixed money mindset. You believe that there's never enough and there never will be.

When you hear those thoughts come into your mind, catch yourself. Stop those thoughts mid-sentence and replace them with something more in line with the growth money mindset. For example:

> 'I never have…' Stop yourself and think, 'I always have enough money to go around.'

Manage Your Mindset

'I'd rather be...' Stop yourself and think, 'I can't wait until I have enough savings to go on that trip.'

'There's always more bills...' Stop yourself and think, 'There's always enough money to pay the bills.'

At first, you'll be surprised at how often you have to stop and catch yourself so that you don't finish that fixed money mindset thought. I know I was. I couldn't believe that I used to think this way every time I had to pay my bills.

But over time, it became a new thought pattern and, consequently, a new way of life.

Make It a Habit

They say that it takes 28 days to make a new habit. Now, I think that depends on your motivation because if you really want something bad enough, you'll make it happen a lot sooner than 28 days.

But let's say that for the next 28 days, you're going to practice thinking and acting like someone with a growth-money mindset.

When you pay your bills, send thanks and praise out to the world for the luxury of having enough money in the bank to pay for everything.

When you put money into your savings, send out love and gratitude because you can do this now.

When you choose to cook instead of spending money on takeaway, give yourself a little pat on the back because you've made a positive choice for your future.

If you do these things often enough, they'll become part of your day-to-day life. They'll be the beginnings of this whole lovely new chapter of your life. The chapter where you're in control, getting stronger and making better choices for yourself.

Later on, we'll dive deeper into creating a positive habit. It's going to make a real difference in your life.

It's Your Turn

Your mindset will determine whether you have a positive money experience or a negative money experience. Changing it and making it work for you is indeed possible.

- ☐ Ask yourself, do I have a fixed money mindset or a growth money mindset?
- ☐ If you have a fixed money mindset, decide today whether you're going to stay that way or change to a growth money mindset.
- ☐ Catch yourself when you start talking or thinking about what you lack or the hardships in your world.
- ☐ For the next 28 days, practice thinking and acting like someone with a growth-money mindset.

CHAPTER FIVE

Nail Your Numbers

One of the things I learnt quickly when I was a sales manager was to know my numbers. Every day, when I would walk into work, my boss would ask for my numbers before I even had a chance to put my handbag on my desk. This is the nature of the sales environment. Everything is hustle and bustle, and numbers and sales. It's a very frantic environment.

Each morning on the train to work, I would review my overnight reports and find my numbers so that I was ready when she saw me coming.

After a few months of this, I think she realised that I knew what I was doing. I had my numbers. I knew where to make small corrections with the team and how to hit our goals.

This is something I've brought into my personal world as well.

I know my numbers.

I know how much is coming in and when it's due to hit my bank account.

I know when each payment is going out and how much each payment is.

I know how much I need to transfer to each bank account every payday.

I know how much I have in my buffer account and how long it's going to take me to reach my savings goal.

Knowing my numbers gives me great comfort. It has removed a lot of the stress and worry from my whole life because this part of my world is managed well.

I have a system I use that makes all of this not just possible but easy. I'll show you the system in a later chapter, but for now, let's look at your numbers.

Finding time to dedicate to this chapter is important—about an hour should do it.

Turn off your phone, the TV, and any other distractions that might interrupt your thoughts so you can use this time to get real about your money situation.

Here's a list of everything you need for this chapter:

- Your payslips for the last month
- Last month's bank statements for every bank account you have
- A calculator
- A notepad (A4 size at a minimum) and pen
- Five coloured highlighter pens

- A cup of coffee or tea or a glass of water
- A box of tissues (just in case things get a bit emotional)

A word of advice...

Take time to get all of this ready before you start the exercises. I promise you that when you get up to get statements or payslips, you'll be distracted by the dust in the corner of the lounge room that you never noticed before. You'll make it your mission to clean it.

This is totally normal and something I've experienced multiple times myself, and so have my clients and other women who have gone through this exercise. Because most of us, at some time or another, have thought that cleaning was way more important than doing our finances. So, if this is you, don't sweat it. You're normal! Today, we're going to up the ante and change your normal into amazing. All in the space of an hour...who'd have thought?!

Ok, you're all set. Let's get to it!

Money Coming In

First, you need to know how much money you have coming in and when it's due to land in your bank account. Now, if you have one job that pays you fortnightly, this is an easy exercise. If you have a few jobs and they each pay you at different intervals, then it might take you a little bit longer, but it's not impossible.

Remember, once you have completed this chapter, you'll feel more in control over your finances than you have in ages, purely because you'll be aware of what's coming in and where it's going. This will empower you to make better decisions.

Step 1:
Grab your latest payslip and write down the salary that went into your bank account and the date of that payment in your notebook. Do this for a whole month. For example, you might have two fortnightly salaries drop into your bank account in a month. Write down both payments.

Repeat this for each job you have until you have a list of all the income you have coming into your bank account for the month.

Step 2:
Write down any other regular payments you may be receiving and the date those payments hit your bank account. These could be things like government payments, rental payments from tenants, income from a business, etc.

Include any regular payments you receive, but not random payments. Payments that happen occasionally we consider a bonus payment, not something you can count on regularly.

Step 3:
Add them up!

Add together each of the payments you have received for the month and write that amount on the page.

Nail Your Numbers

Income	Date	Amount
Pay 1	5 Nov	$2,197
Pay 2	19 Nov	$2,197
Government Payment	28 Nov	$286
Total		**$4,680**

Once you have totalled your incoming payments, you'll know how much money you can expect to receive every month.

Money Going Out

Now that we know how much is coming in, it's equally important to know what's going out. This is where we're going to use your bank statements.

Step 1:
In your notebook, draw a line down the centre of a new page, from top to bottom. At the top of the first column, write 'Expense.' At the top of the second column, write 'Amount.'

Expenses	Amount
Total	

Saving Myself

Step 2:
Grab your first bank statement and, starting at the top, write down the names of all the expenses deducted or paid from your bank account in the Expenses column and the amount of that payment in the Amount column.

Expenses	Amount
Mortgage	$3,358
Groceries	$524
Electricity	$281
Phone	$95
Coffee	$116
Fees and Charges	$15
Total	**$4,389**

Step 3:
Repeat this for each bank account.

Step 4:
Using your highlighter pens, highlight each outgoing payment into one of these categories:

1. **Debts**: mortgage, personal loan, car loan, credit card, student loans, etc. (highlight in orange)
2. **Regular payments**: mortgage or rent, gas, electricity, pay-tv, insurance, subscriptions, mobile phones, etc. (highlight in yellow)
3. **One-off purchases**: shoes, clothing, trinkets, books, food delivery, etc. (highlight in blue)
4. **Daily expenses**: groceries, public transport, a bottle of wine, buying lunch at work, etc. (highlight in pink)
5. **Fees and Charges**: bank transaction fees, late payment fees, etc. (highlight in green)

Of course, you can use whatever colour highlighter pen works for you. I'm just using these colours as a demonstration.

Step 5:
On a clean page of your notebook, make a list of these categories:

- Debts
- Regular Payments
- One-Off Purchases
- Daily Expenses
- Fees and Charges

Categories	Amount
Debts	
Regular Payments	
One-Off Purchases	
Daily Expenses	
Fees & Charges	
Total	

Step 6:
Take your calculator and add up all the payments that have been highlighted in orange. Write this number next to the Debt category. Then, add up all the payments highlighted in yellow. Write this number next to the Regular Payments category. Do the same for One-Off Purchases, Daily Expenses and Fees and Charges.

For example:

- Debt: $2625.46
- Regular Payments: $1653.26
- One-Off Purchases: $296.79

Saving Myself

- Daily Expenses: $516.78
- Fees and Charges: $14.11

Categories	Amount
Debts	$3,358
Regular Payments	$376
One-Off Purchases	$116
Daily Expenses	$524
Fees & Charges	$15
Total	

When each category has an amount next to it, add them all up and write the total at the bottom of the list. You now know where your money is going.

Categories	Amount
Debts	$3,358
Regular Payments	$376
One-Off Purchases	$116
Daily Expenses	$524
Fees & Charges	$15
Total	**$4,389**

You did it!!! I'm so excited for you.

You might not believe it, but you have just completed your first Money Audit. Well done you!

If you already had a good understanding of where your money was going, this will be confirmation that what you're currently doing is working.

If you don't know where your money is going, this exercise will be a real eye-opener. You might find it quite shocking, and you'll start to notice the difference all the $2 spends or the $17 payments made to your bank balance, especially once you add them all up.

Some of my clients have said that this exercise showed them that money was literally disappearing from their bank accounts into a deep, dark hole, leaving them with nothing to show for it at the end of each month.

Others said that it made them feel like their bank accounts were buckets with multiple holes where the money leaked out.

The good news is you can change your situation.

Your Total Net Worth

Your total net worth is one of the most important numbers to know when it comes to understanding your financial situation. It's like getting a full snapshot of your financial health—it tells you exactly where you stand, financially speaking, at any given time.

In simple terms, your total net worth is the difference between what you own (your assets) and what you owe (your liabilities). It's a clear way to measure how much you really have once all debts are accounted for.

To calculate your total net worth, follow these steps:

Step 1:
Start by listing your assets, which is everything you own that has value. This includes:

- Cash in bank accounts
- Retirement Funds
- Investments like shares, bonds, or superannuation
- The value of any properties you own
- Vehicles, jewellery, or other valuable personal items

Add these all together to get the total value of your assets. It looks like this:

Assets	Amount
Cash in Bank Accounts	$5,260
Retirement Funds	$75,329
Investments	$15,160
Property Value	$500,000
Valuable Personal Items	$8,279
Total	**$604,028**

Step 2:
Now, list your liabilities, which is everything you owe. These are your debts and might include:

- Outstanding mortgage balances
- Car loans
- Credit card debt
- Any personal loans

Add these together to get the total value of your liabilities.

It looks like this:

Liabilities	Amount
Mortgage Balance	$300,000
Car Loan	$15,000
Credit Card Debt	$2,500
Personal Loans	$5,000
Total	**$322,500**

Step 3:
Finally, subtract your total liabilities from your total assets. The result is your total net worth.

- For example, if you have $200,000 in assets and $50,000 in liabilities, your net worth is $150,000.

It looks like this:

Total Liabilities - Total Assets = Total Net Worth

$604,028 - $322,500 = $281,528

Total Net Worth = $281,528

Knowing your net worth is essential because it gives you a real-time look at how your finances are doing. While your income and expenses show you the flow of money each month, your net worth shows you the bigger picture of how much wealth (or debt) you've built over time.

By regularly calculating your net worth, you can see whether you're growing your wealth or heading in the wrong direction. It's a powerful tool to help you stay on track and make sure your financial decisions are building toward the life you want.

Your net worth is also an excellent motivator. Watching that number grow, even in small increments, can be a huge confidence boost and a reminder that your efforts are paying off. Even if your net worth is negative right now, knowing where you are allows you to set clear goals to improve it over time.

Remember, your net worth isn't just a number—it's a way to take control, make empowered choices, and build the financial future you deserve.

Your Lifestyle Metric

The next number we're going to talk about is one that isn't often discussed. It's the one that not a lot of people actually know about. It's your Lifestyle Metric.

To put it simply, it's the monthly income you need to earn which will give you breathing room in your life.

So, instead of feeling overwhelmed, financially stressed, and busy all the time, you can sit back, take a breather, and enjoy the financial and lifestyle benefits that all your hard work provides.

Now, let's put some structure around this...

I'm not talking about living lavishly. I'm not talking about diamond studded coffee makers or 24-carat gold tiles in your shower (although I did see a TV show recently where a guy had 24-carat gold tiles throughout his entire ensuite. Not my style, but more power to you if you can pull it off).

I'm also not talking about removing every luxury from your life. I don't want you sitting in the dark with 50 blankets on you in the middle of winter because you don't want to turn on the lights or the heater. (Been there, done that, and I can tell you, it's not a lot of fun.)

What we're looking at here is the amount of money you **need** to have come in that will allow you to live a comfortable lifestyle.

Things like your mortgage or rent, utilities, or debt repayments. How much do you spend on groceries? How much do you spend on your car? Then, add things you like to do for fun.

Here's how we do it...

Step 1:
Using your Money Out list, write down the **essentials only**. These are your must-haves, like your mortgage or rent, food, loan repayments, credit card repayments, or utilities. Write the amount you spend on each of those per month.

Now, we're not including anything non-essential (that will come later, I promise).

Not shoes. Not clothes. Not take-out meals. Not coffee with your girlfriends. Not Netflix. Just the essentials. The things that, if you didn't pay for them, it would mean that you didn't have the necessities of life or your bank manager would send out the debt collectors.

Now, you don't need to start a 300-page spreadsheet to capture all of this. You've got your Money Out list, and it's just a matter of writing down the essentials in your notebook.

It looks like this:

Expense	$ per Month
Mortgage	
Cars/Petrol	
Groceries	
Utilities	
Insurance	

Step 2:
Add up all your essentials, and you'll have a total monthly amount that will allow you to...breathe!!! And we all know that breathing is important, right?

Step 3:
It's highly probable that when you calculate the total of your essentials, it won't be a nice round number. It could be something like $5652.

So, to make your life a little bit simpler, what I want you to do is round that number up to $6000. If it's $7257, I want you to round that up to $8000.

Then, you'll have your very own Lifestyle Metric. (Like I said, we're going back to the basics and building up from there.)

Expense	$ per Month
Mortgage	$3,358
Cars/Petrol	$100
Groceries	$524
Utilities	$281
Insurance	$95
Total	**$4,358**
Round Up	**$4,500**

Once you've got that, you can look at your income and see whether your Lifestyle Metric is more or less than your income. If it's less than your income, thumbs up to you.

Now, you might find out you have more going out than coming in. But this is the beauty of your Lifestyle Metric. It gives you factual information about your financial position, allowing you to make better choices. (Your CFO is high-fiving you right now!)

But don't stress about that now. In the next chapter, I'll show you how to turn your Lifestyle Metric the right way around.

Your Numbers

I have to say I'm impressed. You're still with me and, more importantly, you now know your numbers.

Take a pen and write down the following numbers in your notebook:

- Money In:
- Money Out:

- Total Net Worth:
- Lifestyle Metric:

It looks like this:

Money In:	$3,358
Money Out:	$100
Total Net Worth:	$281,528
Lifestyle Metric:	$4,500

Most importantly, it's time to congratulate yourself and celebrate your wins. Don't overlook the importance of this step. You need to celebrate the wins so that your unconscious mind associates success, all the good feelings it brings to you, and the new life you're building.

It's Your Turn

Knowing your numbers means you stop wandering in the dark and start making informed decisions about your finances. The last thing you want to be doing right now is guessing because it's a surefire way to end up in a worse situation.

- ☐ Set aside an hour
- ☐ Get yourself a cup of tea or coffee or a glass of water
- ☐ Turn off the TV and put your phone on airplane mode
- ☐ Grab everything you need on the list
- ☐ Calculate your money coming in and going out
- ☐ Calculate your Total Net Worth
- ☐ Calculate your Lifestyle Metric
- ☐ Celebrate

CHAPTER SIX

Build Your Budget

Chances are you're not reading this book because everything is hunky-dory in your financial life. You're here because you're worried about your money. It keeps you awake at night, and you want to do something to improve it.

The good news is you've done all the prep work. You've set yourself up for success by choosing to live consciously and having open and honest conversations about money. You've started You Inc. and drawn a line in the sand when it comes to your future. You've looked at your money story and tweaked it to make sure it works for you and your future. You've developed a healthy money mindset and know your numbers.

You've done heaps!

So, let's keep the momentum going and start rebuilding your financial house, beginning with your budget.

For a lot of us, the word budget has a negative connotation. There are a whole bunch of experts who say that YOU MUST BUDGET and others who say BUDGET IS A DIRTY WORD. It's hard to know what to believe.

As you can imagine, I've done a lot of research to find the right formula for me. Through this research, I've come across a lot of different points of view. None bad. None that really hit the spot, either.

I've read that...

- Budgets are restrictive.
- Budgets limit the things you can and can't do.
- Budgets are good in theory but rarely good in practice.

I've seen budgets referred to as *conscious cash flow*, *money management*, and various other things. But when you strip these all back, basically, it's a budget.

I have a bit of a different, albeit simpler, approach to budgeting. I mean, if it's not simple and it's not easy, I'm not likely to do it. You might feel the same.

So, let me tell you how it works in my life.

My budget lets me know how much money I need to have in my accounts each month. How much goes into my household expenses account? How much needs to go into my savings account? How much needs to go into my emergency funds account for my rainy day stuff?

Basically, I get my pay each fortnight. Certain amounts get transferred into each of my accounts for bills and expenses.

Build Your Budget

I have an amount for myself to live on, and the rest goes into savings. That's it. Budget done.

I don't want you to think of a budget as restrictive. I just want you to think of a budget as how much money needs to be here and there so that your bills are paid, your debt is reduced, and your savings are growing.

The purpose of your budget is to help you get clear on what's going on financially.

This isn't the kind of thing you can bury your head in the sand and ignore. I want you to know how much it costs for you to live.

But, if right now the amount it costs for you to live is more than you currently bring in, I don't want you to focus on that. If you focus your energy on what's not working, beating yourself up in the process and having the energy of 'it's not working, it's not working,' you bury yourself in a funky hole and create more of what's not working.

I'm aware of how much money it takes for me to live. I'm aware of it all and this is transforming. All my needs are met. All my desires are fulfilled, and it *feels* amazing.

You deserve to have an amazing life, too. You've earned it.

Here's the best thing: when you've sorted your money, everything else starts to fall into place. So, let's get cracking and build the right budget that works for you.

Declutter

Now that you've completed your first Money Audit and know your numbers, you can start making changes and tweaks to help you begin living life on your own terms but still within your means.

When you look at your first Money Audit, ask yourself, is this how I want my money house to look? Is my Lifestyle Metric more than my Money In? Is there any money left over to save? If your answer is no to any of those questions, we need to do some decluttering.

Remember, to get ahead right now, you may need to go backwards a little bit. What I mean by that is that you may need to cut back on a few luxury items now to get ahead later.

Just remember our philosophy: if you follow your plan and develop positive habits, you'll have a new way of life over time.

We're in the rebuilding phase now and need to start with a solid foundation.

Step 1:
Declutter expert Peter Walsh says, "Clutter, it's not just the stuff on the floor. It's anything that gets between you and the life you want to be living." I think we can apply this to our finances as well.

Go through each of the items on your Money Out list and decide first which items you can get rid of completely. (I love a good red pen to do this bit!)

Put a red cross next to each item that you can absolutely do without. For example, you may have three pay-tv subscriptions but haven't watched any of them for ages. Let's say that you cancel each of your TV subscriptions at $10 each. You have just saved yourself $30 each month, which equals $360 a year back in your pocket...nice!

If you're feeling brave, cross out each one. If you're not ready to go that far, cross out two and leave just one for yourself. But try to challenge yourself to be bold. The more you cut out now, the better you'll feel the next payday (and you might just get some sleep!).

Remember, it's not about living like a pauper. It's about cutting back on a few things now so that you can get ahead later.

Step 2:
Once you have your list of expenses that you can absolutely do without, it's time to cancel them. For some of these, it's a quick jump into your online account to hit unsubscribe, cancel or delete. For others, it might take a little bit more work.

I can promise you that as hard as it is to let some things go, it'll be completely worth it when you see the extra cash in your bank account next month.

Step 3:
Go back and recalculate your Money Out for each of these categories minus the expenses you have just cancelled, deleted, or removed. You'll see where you've made the biggest impact and scored some easy-saving wins.

Step 4:
Check-in with your Lifestyle Metric. Is it closer to being in the black, or do you still need to cut back in some areas? If you do, declutter again.

You may need to do this a few times before you get into a more manageable Lifestyle Metric.

Decluttering has such a cathartic impact on your heart and mind. It feels really good to cancel subscriptions to things you haven't used in ages and may have even forgotten about. And above all else, you're taking back some control, which is the ultimate high to me.

Now, for all the overachievers in the room, if you're feeling really game, you can mark the items you would like to cut back on. Instead of buying lunch every day at work, take your lunch to work Monday to Thursday and have Friday as a special day to splurge on lunch. This will help you shave back your expenses and have more money in your cash flow.

One thing to remember here is that you're not necessarily taking big cuts to your expenses. You're making small, imperfect steps towards your future by shaving back small amounts of money, allowing you to regain control of your finances.

Your Bank Accounts

Full confession...this is my favourite part!!!

I'm going to share with you how I set up my bank accounts and create my budget. A lot of people can overcomplicate this part, which means they're reluctant to roll up their sleeves and get it done.

And if you know me, you know that I don't do complicated. I have a busy brain, and I need to use it wisely so anything too difficult just doesn't happen.

Build Your Budget

As we have already established, a budget is a simple thing. Basically, it's deciding when your money comes in, how you want it to go out and how much you want to keep.

But when you mention budgets to people, you can see their eyes glaze over, and their attention spans evaporate. People just aren't interested, which absolutely blows my brain.

But not you…

You're savvy about your money and in control of your future. You know that your budget is one of the biggest tools you use to manage your finances. And your budget happens on auto-pilot. #winningatlife

Oh, and when we're talking about our Savvy Philosophy, this is the planning part. The positive habits part comes a bit later when we automate.

I have four bank accounts:

- Splurge
- Household Expenses
- Catastrophe
- Savvy Smile

My Splurge Account is mine—all mine!
It's for me to do whatever the heck I want. However, it has to pay for any food, including my weekly groceries, clothes, shoes, stationery, books, knick-knacks, public transport, coffee with friends, dinners out, and drinks after work on Friday. It's the account that lets me live the lifestyle I want...as long as I can afford it.

My Household Expenses Account is my Adult Account
This is the account that handles all my regular payments. Mortgage or rent, utilities (electricity, gas, water), insurance (home, contents, car, personal), subscriptions (pay-tv, magazines, books), and phones (internet, mobile).

My Catastrophe Account is my Emergency Account
This account is the 'break glass in case of emergency' account. This is the account for emergencies only. I played around with a few different names for this one—my *Can't Sleep Account*, Meltdown Account, or *Put Out The Fire Account*. But none of them felt right until I came up with my *Catastrophe Account*. I only touch it in the case of an absolute catastrophe. What I wanted to do with this one was make sure that the name stopped me from dipping into it just to buy something that looked or felt good.

My Savvy Smile Account is my Savings Account
Whenever I look at this account, it just makes me smile. I can't help it. This is the money that sits in my account and works for me. It has a higher interest rate than the others, so my money is earning me money, and that feels good. This is the account that I use to save up for big things I want, like a new car, a holiday, or even a deposit on a house.

Create Your Buckets

I used to be fanatical about checking my bank accounts every day because I had to be. It was always a juggle and always a struggle.

I would *need* to check my credit card daily (sometimes multiple times a day) to make sure it wasn't overdrawn. If it was, I would have to take money from another account to cover it so that I didn't get charged extra fees I couldn't afford. Then, the other account would be less than I needed, and I would have to find a way to juggle that or simply go without. I was so close to the wire that it kept me awake every night.

Now, it's a breeze.

Because I know my numbers, I know how much it costs me to live daily. I know how much I can afford to put into my savings. I've also been able to build up my emergency account to a point where I could take a year off and still live the lifestyle I'm living today.

It's super exciting.

Here's how I set up my bank accounts…

My Household Expenses, Catastrophe, and Savvy Smile accounts are with one bank, and my Splurge account is with a completely separate bank. The reason is to stop me from transferring money from one of my three automated accounts to my Splurge account. (It would be too easy if it was in the same bank).

I set up three accounts with the first bank (I chose an online bank because their fees are lower and it's easy to set up online—it took me all of ten minutes) and one account with the second bank (I chose one of the Big Four banks for this one).

In the online bank, the first account I set up was a zero-fee everyday transaction account. I also set up two high-interest online savings accounts (the ones that give you bonus interest when you don't make any withdrawals).

I named the everyday transaction account My Household Expenses.

I named one of the high-interest accounts My Catastrophe Account and the other high-interest account My Savvy Smile.

This is what it looks like:

In the second bank, I already had an everyday transaction account. So I used that one and renamed it 'Splurge.'

I have deliberately set it up this way so I'm not tempted to transfer money from the automated accounts into my Splurge account. I only have to check my automated accounts once a week or on payday because I know they're all set up and working correctly.

Mortgages, loans, and credit cards

"But Jo, what about my mortgage and my loans or credit cards?" Don't worry; we've got them sorted, too.

Now, depending on your pay cycle, you might have to do a bit of juggling at the start to get this sorted, but it won't be too hard. My personal loan was a monthly repayment (due to an error by the personal banker—thanks, dude!), and my wages were paid fortnightly. But I managed to sort it out.

There are a couple of ways that you can do this.

1. You can create an automatic payment from your pay directly into your loan account.
2. You can include the repayments in your total household expenses and then create a direct debit to your loan/credit card.
3. You can manually make the payment.

We'll talk about this a bit more when we automate your finances and eliminate stress.

Make It Automatic

One of my favourite things about my business is that I have a fantastic payroll system that allows me and my team to allocate our pay into any number of bank accounts automatically. (This is so cool; you're going to love it!)

Because I know my numbers, I know how much money I need to have in my Household Expenses account to pay my bills each month, how much I can add to my Catastrophe account, and how much I can save in my Savvy Smile account.

So, what I do is add each of my bank accounts to my HR/payroll profile and determine from my money out how much I want to go into each account on payday.

For example:

1. Household expenses account: I have half my monthly expenses paid into this account. For those two months a year when we have three fortnightly payments in a month, I leave them in this bank account because it creates an amazing buffer just in case anything changes.
2. Catastrophe account: I have set a payment into that account each pay.
3. Savvy Smile account: I have 10% of my whole pay transferred into this account.
4. Splurge account: I have the balance of my pay transferred to my Splurge Account.

Note:

Depending on where you have your mortgage or loans, you can set up an allocation of your pay directly into those accounts as well. That way, it's completely seamless. Or you can include them in your Household Expenses account and set up a direct debit to your loan accounts.

Now, if this isn't possible (because not every payroll system is set up this way), you can create automatic payments through your bank.

I recommend you have your salary or wages paid to your Splurge Account. From there, you can set up automatic payments to the other accounts. It's still automatic; you just have to be diligent and not go on a spending spree on payday. But I know you can do it.

Build Your Budget

It's Your Turn

Automating your budget takes the stress and worry out of payday. Instead of freaking out each payday, you monitor and tweak your accounts and payday payments and enjoy the time you used to spend stressing about your bills.

- ☐ Declutter like a crazy person
- ☐ Create your buckets
- ☐ Make it automatic
- ☐ Celebrate this huge milestone!

CHAPTER SEVEN

Demolish Your Debt

Debt. It's a word that strikes fear into the hearts of many…or so it goes.

I think I've lived with debt most of my adult life. I've had good debt (my home loan) and bad debt (personal loans and credit cards). For me, they were a way of life.

Or at least they used to be.

Imagining a life without debt was hard at the start. I mean, I had dreamt of being debt-free for years and years *and years*. I imagined having spare money and holidays and upgrading my car when I was debt-free, but there was always one thing that niggled at me. That was, what do you do when an emergency hits and you don't have a credit card to fall back on?

The answer: your *Catastrophe Account*!

This was a huge shift for me in my way of thinking about and managing my money.

I have paid off my credit cards more times than I can tell you, only to have them climb back up to their limit. Why is this? Because I struggled with impulse control and I was an emotional spender.

Whenever I would argue with my ex-husband or an ex-partner, I would whip out the credit card, shop, and feel better afterward. Well, at least until the next credit card bill came in and I could only afford to pay the minimum.

I have refinanced my debt and consolidated it into one loan, too. More than once.

I think it's safe to say that I was on the debt seesaw and couldn't find a way to get off.

Until…I made a decision.

I decided I was tired of chasing my financial tail and of the stress and worry of managing my debt. I wasn't sleeping. I wasn't happy. I wasn't living the life I deserved. Because I wasn't managing my money anymore, I was spending most of my time managing my debt. The bad kind. I wasn't getting ahead. I wasn't making my life better. I was going in the opposite direction to the one I really wanted to go.

While my friends were going on holidays, I was at home checking my online banking multiple times a day to make sure that I didn't overdraw on my credit cards. I was juggling my accounts like a crazy person.

Then, one day, I decided I had enough of this lifestyle (which wasn't really a lifestyle at all). I decided I was going to be debt-free, and I was going to do it as fast as humanly possible.

Change Your Mind About Debt

The ability to become debt-free isn't dependent on your income. It's all about changing your mind and behaviour and being really focused and intense about getting rid of your debt.

To some extent, it's about living like a grown-up, and I know how confronting this statement is.

I consider myself to be a responsible grown-up. I have a reasonable amount of intelligence (not a Rhodes Scholar by any stretch of the imagination, but I can hold my own at any pub trivia night). I'm capable (hello…single mother of four here). I'm savvy (give me a paperclip, some sticky tape, and a metre of string, and I'll pull a MacGyver and build you a windmill—not really, but you get my drift).

But when it came to money, I was an irresponsible person. And that hurts me to say, even today (deep breath, Jo).

But I was smart enough to know that if I didn't change my behaviour, my debt would continue to seesaw, and I would never get ahead in this world. I also knew I had a finite time to work and bring in an income. With each day ticking down and my debt growing, I was going backward.

So, I changed my mind about debt. I changed my mind about spending my time managing my debt instead of my money. I decided to focus on nothing else other than eliminating my debt. Right then. Right there.

Saving Myself

As Dave Ramsay says, "To the exclusion of virtually everything else, I am getting out of debt."

I took Dave's quote, printed it several times and posted copies of it around my house. On my fridge. On the back of the toilet door. I even put it in a frame and placed it on my dressing table so it was the first thing I saw every day.

I changed my mind about money and decided I wasn't going to feel trapped by debt anymore. I was going to liberate myself and remove debt from my life. Not just for now but forever.

Make a List

The first thing I did was make a list of all my debts and the amount I owed on each one. Everything from my credit cards to my personal loans, to my payment plans, and anything in between. I listed anything I owed to someone or some business on my notepad.

And then I cried.

I had managed to get myself into a really bad situation. I had over $40,000 worth of personal debt—the bad kind—and I had practically nothing to show for it. I also had an income of $50,000 per year. The maths just didn't work.

So, I decided that the best course of action here was to cry. Cry until there were no more tears left to cry. It took a little while (maybe 30 minutes or so). But once the tears had dried up and the shock and emotion had passed through me, my brain switched back on, and I got busy making a plan.

Remember our Savvy Philosophy—a solid plan plus good positive habits over time equals a new way of life!

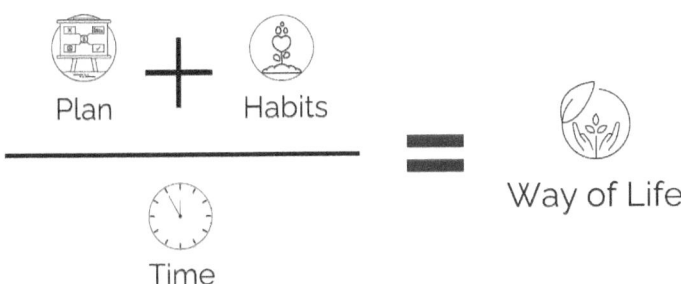

Take Some Interest

The next thing I did was conduct a little bit of research. I found out what the interest rate was for each of my debts.

Also, another shocking activity.

Each of my credit cards was at 24.99% interest. That meant I was paying a quarter of the balance, on top of the balance, to the bank for the privilege of using their credit card. Insane, I know!!

My personal loan was at 13.95%. No wonder I was drowning.

On my notepad, I had a list of all my debts (including the amount I owed) and wrote down the interest rate for each one next to it.

I also added a column for the minimum repayment for each debt.

Debt	Owed	Interest	Min
Credit Card	$5,267	19.95%	$108
Store Card	$2,189	24.99%	$56
Car Loan	$5,693	4.74%	$304
Personal Loan	$4,859	4.99%	$145

Now that I had all the facts, I could make better decisions. I put myself back in the driver's seat and started managing my money and paying off my debt.

Debt Me Out of Here

The strategy I used to get myself out of debt is simple on paper but a little challenging on the mind. It's going to take some mental toughness and commitment to make this happen. I want to call this out now so you're prepared for the tricks your mind and emotions will play on you as you get yourself out of debt.

But I know you're a savvy woman, and I know you can do this. After all, you wouldn't have read this far if you weren't.

If I'm honest with myself, I know that I'm hopeless when it comes to credit cards. Even today, I know I'm an emotional spender, and I had a lot of emotions to contend with back then. It just made sense to get rid of all the credit cards as quickly as possible.

To do this, I had to move my direct debits for my phone, internet, utilities, and any other regular payments to my Household

Expenses account. (If you didn't do this when you were automating your buckets, now is a good time to get this done.)

Trust me, the frequent flier points I earned for having all these payments on my credit card were nothing compared to the control I have over my spending habits now. What I could have saved on a flight when I cashed in my points, I can pay 10 times in cash now and not have the debt around my neck.

Once that was done, I cut up my credit cards. Scary, *yes*, but totally worth it! I knew that if I had them in my possession, I would be tempted to use them, and I would never get myself out of debt. Remember what I said earlier—the hard part is in the mind—this is that moment.

The next thing I did was re-write my list of debts from smallest to biggest. The reason I listed everything that way was to get some quick wins under my belt. I needed proof (consciously and unconsciously) that my plan was going to work.

I stuck this list on my fridge so that I could see it every day. I didn't want it locked away in a notepad somewhere where I could forget about it. I wanted it in my face! I wanted to feel sick when I saw it. I wanted to feel motivated to demolish it.

Now that I had my list, I was ready to debt the hell out of there!

There are two common debt reduction strategies that you may have heard of. One is the Debt Snowball Plan. The other is the Debt Avalanche Plan.

The *Debt Avalanche Plan* involves making minimum payments on all your outstanding accounts and then using any of the remaining money earmarked for your debts to pay off the bill with the highest interest rate. Using the debt avalanche method will save you the most in interest payments.

The *Debt Snowball Plan* involves paying off the smallest debts first to get them out of the way before moving on to bigger ones—kind of a "tackle the easy jobs first" approach. You make a list of all the outstanding amounts you owe in descending order. You target the first one to pay off, putting as much extra money into each payment as you can afford. For the others, you pay just the minimum. When the first debt is settled, you target the next-smallest one for the extra-payment treatment.

In addition to these methods, there's another approach I like to call the *Heart Repayment Plan*. This strategy focuses not on the size of the debt or the interest rate but on the emotional weight each debt carries. The first debt you pay off is the one that causes you the most hurt, upset, or stress. Maybe it's the one that reminds you of a difficult time or a mistake that's been hanging over you for too long. Once you clear that debt, you'll feel an emotional release, and then you move on to the next debt that weighs heavily on your heart.

The idea behind the Heart Repayment Plan is that by tackling the debts that cause the most emotional pain first, you'll experience a sense of relief and motivation to keep going. Paying off each painful debt helps to lift the emotional burden and creates momentum as you begin to feel lighter and more in control with each one that disappears. Keep going until you've cleared all the debts that have been holding you back.

For me, the Heart Repayment Plan suited me best because it allowed me to free myself from the debts that caused me the most stress. I didn't start with the smallest debt or the highest interest rate—I started with the one that weighed on me emotionally. The one that made me feel the worst. I made the minimum payments on all my debts except for that one, and I threw as much money as I possibly could at it until it was paid off.

Once I cleared that emotionally heavy debt, I felt such a sense of relief. I then took the money I had been using for that debt and applied it to the next one that caused me pain. Each time I crossed a debt off my list, it felt like I was lightening the load on my heart. With every painful debt I paid off, my motivation grew stronger.

By the time I reached my last and biggest debt, I was paying off large amounts at once, demolishing it much faster than I had imagined. The emotional weight lifted with each debt I paid off, and it was incredible. I felt empowered every time I got to cross one more off the list taped to my fridge. It wasn't just about becoming debt-free but healing myself along the way.

I'm happy to tell you that the day I did this activity was when I changed my life's direction.

I knew that I had to do something about my debt. If I kept going this way, I knew it was highly likely that I would end up bankrupt or even worse.

So I decided, right then and there, that I was going to get myself out of debt and not go there again. And I haven't. I no longer have debt and have grown my financial house to something my wildest dreams couldn't have imagined.

It's Your Turn

Let's debt you the hell out of there:

- ☐ Grab your pen and notebook and write down your debts from smallest to largest.
- ☐ Next to each debt, write down the total amount you owe and the minimum payment amount.
- ☐ Write down the interest rate for each debt.
- ☐ Cut up your credit card (you can do it. I believe in you).
- ☐ Decide on the debt reduction strategy that works best for you.
- ☐ Demolish the rest of your debt.
- ☐ Celebrate your win!

CHAPTER EIGHT

Nourish Your Nest Egg

The nest egg. That magical golden egg that sits on a nest of a mythical bird in our fairy tales. It's the thing that Jack risked his life and climbed the beanstalk for. It's the thing that we talk about, but do we really know much about it that isn't wrapped in a fairy tale?

The term 'nest egg' has been used to refer to savings since the late 17th century and is believed to have been derived literally from poultry farmers' tactic of placing eggs—both real and fake—in hens' nests to encourage them to lay more eggs which meant more income for the farmers.

In today's reality, a nest egg is a substantial amount of money or assets that have been saved or invested for a specific purpose, usually retirement.

Now, this could also include things like buying a home for yourself, putting the kids through university, or buying that investment property.

It can also be money that's kept aside as a reserve to deal with life's unexpected emergencies, like car repairs, a leaky roof, or an unexpected health problem.

There's no one-size-fits-all approach to establishing your nest egg. Different financial experts will tell you you need a $1 million nest egg to comfortably retire. Others will tell you something different. Depends on who you listen to, I guess.

What I'm about to do is share with you something that will have the financial purists up in arms and flapping about like crazy people. I'm going to take creative licence with the whole nest egg concept and adapt it for our benefit. (I know, crazy, right??)

I believe that it's critical to build several nest eggs. This will allow you to retire comfortably, not rely solely on government benefits and achieve your financial goals, like buying your own home. It will also allow you to make sure you have enough money set aside for when the car breaks down or the roof springs a leak.

As we're focusing on rebuilding our financial house, we will work backward and start by ensuring we have an 'In Case Of Emergency' Nest Egg…aka our Catastrophe Account.

Catastrophe Account

As we touched on earlier, your Catastrophe Account (your emergency fund) is a separate savings account used to cover the expense of unforeseen situations.

Emergencies, by definition, are unpredictable. When they happen, it's usually at the worst possible time and can derail your entire financial house.

A sudden illness, accident, or unexpected job loss can devastate your cash flow and put a massive hole in your savings.

While emergencies can't always be avoided, mitigating the risk by having emergency savings can take the sting out.

The size of your emergency fund will vary depending on your lifestyle, monthly costs, and income. The rule of thumb is to put away at least three to six months' worth of expenses. This amount can seem daunting at first, but the idea is to put a small amount away each payday to build up to that goal.

Your emergency savings should be placed in an account that's easily accessible so you don't incur any early penalties if you need to access it. Think back to the Build Your Buckets chapter. We created a savings account and called it our Catastrophe Account (you may have named it something else, which is completely okay. Whatever works for you is what I want you to do).

If you go back to your notebook, where you calculated your numbers, you'll know how much money you need to have each month to keep your head above water.

Take that number and multiply it by three (or six if you're feeling game). This is the number you need to put into your emergency account in case of an unforeseen event.

When you go back and look at your budget, is there any wriggle room to start putting money into your emergency account? It doesn't have to be huge amounts of cash. It can be anything, as long as it's regularly going into your emergency account.

Now, you may be asking yourself, do I pay off my debts or build my emergency funds first?

Honestly, it's entirely up to you which one you do first.

If you get more comfort and sleep easier by having built your emergency funds first, then do that. But just keep in mind that you're paying interest on your debts, which is eating away at your cash flow each and every day. If this sits well with you, then the emergency fund it is.

If you'd prefer to demolish your debts first, then that's what you choose. Either way, you're making progress and rebuilding your financial house.

For me, it was more important and allowed me to sleep better when I had emergency funds in my account. There was something very peaceful about having money to draw on in an emergency that wouldn't set me back financially and stop me from moving ahead. Once I had this, I then focused on demolishing my debts.

That strategy worked for me. I encourage you to follow the strategy that works for you.

Short-Term Goals

One of the things I love about short-term goals is they allow you to get a few quick wins under your belt.

Achieving some quick wins gives evidence to your unconscious mind that your plan works. It convinces your fears and worries that this can be done and, therefore, quiets the mind and opens it up to possibilities.

Nourish Your Nest Egg

Your short-term goals can be something like getting the couch re-covered or putting that veggie patch in the backyard. You're a brunette, and now you want to be a blonde (this was one of my favourites that I did). Maybe you want to go on a weekend away with the girls at the end of the year.

I like to think of short-term goals as anything I want to accomplish in the next 12 months. It doesn't have to take the whole 12 months to achieve. It could be something you want to do in six months, three months, or even a few weeks.

That's the beauty of short-term goals. This is the fun playground where grown-ups get to folly around and get up to some healthy, let their hair down, and stomp in the puddles kind of fun that we deny ourselves all too often.

One of the best short-term goals I ever set my sights on was taking a whole month off work and renting an Airbnb in regional Victoria. I was a contractor at the time, which meant that if I wasn't working, I wasn't getting paid. But I knew my numbers. I knew how much I would need to keep my household expenses going if I wasn't working. I did my research and knew how much I would need to rent a property for a whole month. With these numbers, I knew how much I needed to save. Spread that over the 12-month period, and I was good to go.

I had the absolute best time. The fresh air. The birds. The trees. I recharged my batteries and felt amazing. I cooked (I know...not normally my thing, but hey, fresh air will do that to you). I wrote in my journal. I read books. I meditated. I sat, and I listened. I was present. I was resting. It was beautiful and something that I'll remember forever.

So, your job now is to choose your very own goal that you want to breathe life into over the next 12 months.

Make a list of everything that comes to mind. If you run out of ideas, wait a minute or two, and your mind will literally spill out another list of ideas. Wait another minute or two, and it'll do it again. It usually takes three goes at this before you get everything on paper. (Don't forget that you can keep adding to it at any time).

Then, pick one—it's that simple!!

Pick your goal, pick a date, then put it on your fridge. Create a plan of how you're going to make it happen. List the resources you need and, most importantly, get going!

I promise you'll feel like you're walking on air when you complete your first goal. It's an amazing feeling and rather addictive.

Long-Term Goals (Your Actual Nest Egg)

This is the adulting part of the whole nest egg strategy.

This is the part where you sit down and actually work out where you want to be in the next 10, 20, 30, or more years. What type of lifestyle do you want to be living? If you're renting, has it always been your dream to have your own home? If you've always wanted to pack up and travel the world, is now the time to do that? If you want to retire well and not be reliant on government pensions, now is the time to put that plan in place.

Your long-term financial goals are usually goals that take several years or even decades to reach. They generally tick along in the background of our lives as we're busy doing the day-to-day things.

Once you have identified your long-term goals, it's about working out your numbers and saving accordingly.

I'm going to assume that you've demolished all your debt, which will free you up financially to budget and save for your long-term goals. Of course, if you're ambitious and want to do it all at once, more power to you. Just remember that laser focus is the best kind of focus. Paying off that debt first will give you more money in the bank than any pay raise your boss could give you.

Find a safe place to store your nest egg until you need it. This is the moment that you get yourself an appointment with a financial planner. They are the best ones to help you plan for your future. Shop around for a financial planner who has a similar mindset to you. They'll be your money partner going forward, and that relationship needs to be easy and comfortable for you.

Don't be afraid to say no to a financial planner you don't gel with. There are plenty out there for you to choose from.

Ask around for referrals. If there's one thing I know, people love talking about their successes and referring good people to good people.

Leave a Legacy

Ask yourself how you want your friends and family to remember you when you're gone.

Most people don't ask themselves this question until it's way too late, and there's not enough time to do anything about it. But we're going to talk about it now.

Your legacy is the impact you make on those who outlive you. Most of the time, it's an inheritance, such as money or property. But it's not always limited to those two things.

A legacy is an opportunity for you to change the world for your family for good. It gives you the opportunity to live for a purpose that's bigger than yourself. It allows you to change your family tree for generations to come.

My kids have watched me struggle financially for most of their life. They've also watched me turn that around and have seen me rebuild my financial house to the point where I even shock myself some days when I check my accounts. I've become a positive financial role model for my children, and they'll pass that down to their children and so on. This is part of my legacy.

My hope and dream is that when I pass over to the other side, I will leave my family enough of an inheritance to positively change their lives. I get comfort from the fact that I have taught them the value of money and how to manage it well so that it works in partnership with them.

Once again, I'm not a legal expert, but I strongly encourage you to get some proper advice and ensure that your wishes and the rights of your nearest and dearests are taken care of by making sure that you have a legally binding will in place. This is your safeguard when it comes to transitioning your wealth and leaving a legacy that will live on long after you have gone.

It's Your Turn

Planning for your future is the opportunity for you to dream and imagine. It gives your life direction and helps you build a lifestyle that lets you live from your heart.

- ☐ Build your Catastrophe Account
- ☐ List your short-term goals and pick one to get started on
- ☐ List your long-term goals and find a financial planner to help you and give you the right advice
- ☐ Ask yourself how you want to be remembered when you're gone, and make sure that you have a legally binding will in place

CHAPTER NINE

Hone Your Habits

Whether you realise it or not, your life has been and will continue to be, created by your habits. Those little things that you do repeatedly, without thought or concern.

Because we do them on an unconscious level, we're not always aware that we're doing them and are often oblivious to the consequences.

Or we might have conscious awareness of them, but the pull toward the habit is so strong that we struggle to fight the urge and often give in to our desires.

According to the Merriam-Webster dictionary,

> *A habit is a usual way of behaving, an acquired mode of behaviour that has become nearly or completely involuntary, a behaviour pattern acquired by frequent repetition or physiologic exposure that shows itself in regularity or increased facility of performance.*

Basically, that means that habits are the behaviours we repeat over and over again without having to be consciously prompted or having to think about them.

Mahatma Gandhi says,

> *Your beliefs become your thoughts, your thoughts become your words, your words become your actions, your actions become your habits, your habits become your values, your values become your destiny.*

Your current life has been created from the sum of all of your habits. What you do repeatedly ultimately forms the person you are, the things you believe, and the personality you portray. When you learn to transform your habits, you learn how to change your life.

Remember our formula:

> *A good plan plus positive habits, over time, creates a new way of life.*

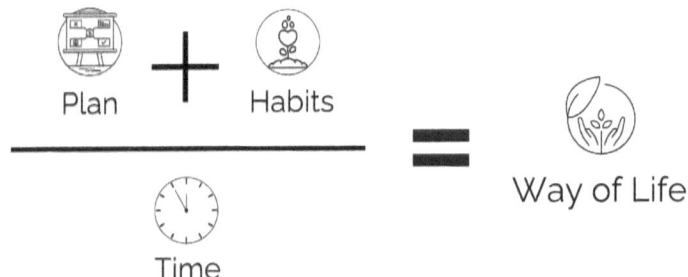

Up until now, we've been working on your plan. You have a budget that you've made automatic. You have a plan to 'debt me out of here,' and you also have your savings goals in place.

Hone Your Habits

PLAN = BIG TICK!

So, the first part of our formula is complete.

A lot of people, in fact, the majority of the population, stop at this part. They don't take the next step. They believe that a plan is enough to change their life. But a plan without positive habits to reinforce it is like planting a beautiful garden but not watering it, removing the weeds, or fertilising it and expecting it to grow, flourish and look amazing in a year's time. It's just not going to happen.

To set you up for complete success, we're going to support your plan by creating some habits and then showing you how to make them stick!

Impulse Spending

Let's start with talking about the Achilles heel that most of us have—impulse spending.

Impulse spending is one of those things that seem so important at the time but end up leaving us feeling guilty, broke, and sometimes even in tears.

It's like it's a crazy bug that bites you and gets you to do things that just don't make sense on paper.

So, if we're going to change our financial circumstances and put some positive habits in place to support our plan, we first need to create a new habit around our impulse spending.

Saving Myself

There are three main reasons that people impulse buy:

- Emotions
- Past experiences
- The perception that we're getting a good deal

Our emotions play a huge part in what we buy and when. So, when you're having a bad day, a little retail therapy can be just the thing that makes you feel better. Maybe it's just a new pair of earrings, something nice for the kitchen or a top that catches your eye as you walk past the shop window.

You tell yourself that it's not a big deal. It doesn't seem too expensive. You just want something nice to make you feel better. It's been a tough day, and you deserve it.

Sound familiar?

Making decisions when you're feeling emotional is a surefire way to let impulse buying take over your life. Particularly in the early stages of your money journey when there's a lot of uncertainty, raw emotion, and vulnerability.

And don't forget that advertisers play on these emotions. Somehow, they seem to know your thoughts and feelings and convince you through images of sunsets and happily ever afters that you cannot possibly go on without their product. Then out comes the credit card…you know what I'm saying, right?

If impulse buying and overspending have been problematic for you forever, chances are you were never taught how to manage money well (think about your money story), and you might have some limiting beliefs about money (think about your money mindset).

Hone Your Habits

You learned your money habits from your family and early childhood experiences. Revisit the earlier chapters for help with changing your story and mindset.

Hands up, who loves a good sale?

Let's be honest, we all do. We love the thought that buying things on special or at a discounted rate makes that purchase so much more justifiable.

I mean, who can blame you when you buy two pairs of shoes because you'll save 50% on the second pair? BARGAIN!!!!

I'm a sucker for a book (thank you, Amazon). I can buy a book, and it will land on my doorstep the next day. It's like magic. Then I take that book, unpack it, hold it to my chest like it's my most prized possession, bask in that feeling for a few moments, and pop it on the bookcase with all the other books I bought but haven't had time to read (ironic, isn't it??).

It's been said that more than half of women impulse buy because of a sale. This is a marketing tactic, and we're all susceptible to it.

So, how do you stop impulse buying and stick to your plan?

Well, for starters, we've done some of the work already.

- We have a budget, and we have automated it…tick
- We have our Splurge Account where we can buy whatever the heck we want…tick

Here are some tips and tricks to help you when the gremlin of impulse spending gets fed after midnight:

Saving Myself

- Give yourself a day or two to calm down before you make your purchase. Then, ask yourself if you'll actually use the purchase and if there's enough money in your Splurge Account to buy it.
- Shop with a plan in mind. Before you leave the house, decide what items you want to buy and how much you want to spend.
- Declutter your email list. One, two, three clicks, and your cart is full of sale items you wouldn't even know about without that email. Unsubscribe from all the sales emails and narrow your focus to your plan and goals.
- Don't go shopping when you're emotional. This can apply to happy and sad emotions. I know that I'll spend just as much when I'm on a high as when I'm feeling low. The roller coaster of emotions can be a very expensive ride.
- Leave the cards at home and only use cash. Work out how much you need and take that amount out in cash. If you stick to your shopping plan, you can't make an impulse buy when the cash runs out.
- You're in the process of up-levelling your life. So, when something piques your interest, and you're thinking that you simply must have it, ask yourself, does this choice help me up-level my life? Buying impulsively and overspending will eat away any extra money you were saving towards your goals. All that hard work and sacrifice you made earlier will be for nothing if you buy that outfit that will probably sit in your wardrobe with the tag on for months, if not years, until you declutter again. If it doesn't help you up-level your life, it doesn't get purchased.

Hone Your Habits

Create a New Habit

As I said earlier, where you are now is a result of the habits you've formed over a lifetime. Whether it be your weight, career, or finances, your current situation is formed by your habits—good or bad.

One of the biggest obstacles that people face when they want to change a part of their life, or their whole life, for the better, is that they don't have a strategy to support them. They don't know what to expect and aren't ready for the mental and emotional challenges that are part and parcel of implementing a new habit.

The question then is, how do I become the master of my financial habits? How do I take complete control of my money and, ultimately, my future?

You do this by learning how to identify, implement and sustain positive habits and permanently remove any negative ones.

In the book *The Miracle Morning* by Hal Elrod, Hal tells us that there are three stages that we go through when implementing new habits:

- Stage 1: Days 1 to 10
- Stage 2: Days 11 to 20
- Stage 3: Days 21 to 30

He calls Stage 1 *Unbearable*. It's the first ten days of implementing a new habit. He says that as the newness and excitement of the new habit wears off (usually by day three), it's replaced by rejection and resistance. Your mind tells you, 'I don't like how this feels,' so you want to stop. Most people give up here and never create the change they want in their life. What they don't realise is that this stage is only temporary.

He calls Stage 2 *Uncomfortable*. The second 10 days are easier because you're getting used to your new habit. It's also where you've developed some confidence and positive associations with the benefits of your new habit.

He calls Stage 3 *Unstoppable*. The final 10 days are when you begin sustaining your new habit long-term. It's when you positively reinforce and associate pleasure with your new habit. It's when your new habit becomes part of your identity. It stops being something you're trying to do and forms part of who you are.

As you can see, each stage represents a set of emotional and mental challenges we go through when creating a new habit.

Let's apply this now to our plan and create new habits, pay cycle by pay cycle.

Your First Pay Cycle

As we just learnt, the first few days of a new habit are the easiest because you're excited and know you're doing something positive for yourself and your future. But when the newness wears off, reality sets in, you realise there are sacrifices you need to make, and you become acutely aware that 'the struggle is real.'

It's like when you decide you're going to get up half an hour earlier in the morning and go for a 30-minute walk. The alarm goes off the first day, and you jump out of bed. Your walking clothes are ready, and your shoes are there. You're on fire and ready to go!

On the third day, you're still pumped, but you hit the snooze button just once, and then you hop out of bed and go on your walk.

Hone Your Habits

Day five, you're doing ok, but you hit that snooze button twice.

Day seven, you don't worry about the snooze button; you just go straight to the alarm, turn it off and pull the covers back for a bit more sleep. And who can blame you…it's cold out there and toasty warm under the blankets. Anyone would do the same in this situation, right??

The good news here (in fact, it's great news) is that this part is temporary!

Most people associate getting out of bed 30 minutes earlier with sleep deprivation, cold weather, and the snooze button. They believe that this is how it's going to be when you adopt this new habit long-term, so it's no wonder they hide under the covers when the alarm goes off.

But what they don't realise is that this is short-term pain for long-term gain.

So, let's put this in our terms.

You have your automated budget, and your first payday hits your bank. As planned, your pay is distributed to each of your accounts (just like we talked about) and it looks so pretty.

You have your Splurge Account and it's ready for you to buy whatever the heck you want.

You have your Household Expenses account, and your bills and regular expenses are set to come out of it.

You have tucked a little bit away in your Catastrophe Account.

Saving Myself

You have executed operation 'Debt Me Out Of Here' and paid off some debts.

You. Are. On. Fire.

You're high-fiving yourself like a crazy person. And you celebrate the fact that it worked, and you're working it!!

Then, it happens…you see it…in the window…that thing…that one thing you cannot live the rest of your life without. You know the one…it has a secret song that only you can hear…it's whispering to you…'you need me'…'you want me'…'you must have me'…

But your mind tells you, 'WAIT! We've just gone through all the trouble of setting up our budget, and everything is on track to pay off our debt and get ourselves right side up in our life.'

The urge is strong…must…not…give…in!

But it's so pretty…must…have…it!

Your mind says, 'If we buy this, it will wipe out our Splurge Account, and we'll have nothing else to live on until the next pay.'

The secret song that gets into your heart tells you, 'It's ok…you have money in other accounts…no one will know…you have to have me.'

Sound familiar?

Well, this is how it plays out in my mind anyway…

Resisting the urge to stop following the plan is real! It's not a sign of weakness. It's not a lack of ability. It's simply your old habits trying to survive.

But this habit is no longer serving you, which is why we're implementing a new one.

The key to your first payday success is being prepared. You know that the first payday can be challenging and will test you. You also know that it's temporary.

So what can you do between now and your next pay that'll help you resist temptation?

Could it be that you don't go to the shops in the first 10 days?

Could you shop for groceries online and keep an eye on how much they cost so you don't blow your budget in one shop?

Whatever strategy you put in place for the first pay cycle, you know you're strong, capable, and determined enough to persist and persevere through this.

And it's only one pay cycle.

Your Second Pay Cycle

Now that you've made it through your first pay cycle (double high five to you 🙌), the second pay cycle is a little bit easier.

Your second pay has now hit your account. The plan has worked, and your pay has been disbursed to your accounts. You're watching your Catastrophe Account grow and your debt reduce. Your Splurge Account just got a new injection of funds, and your household expenses are ticking along nicely in the background. You're killing it!

But…you still have to be mindful of the little gremlin that tries to entice you into blowing out your budget. It will still be tempting to go back to the way it was before you picked up this book, but you have more control now.

If you need more motivation, remember how you felt before opening this book. How hard it was to get through each day, and how troubled you felt each time your pay hit your account. You don't want to go back there. You have put in so much work and effort to set yourself up for your future. Don't undo all that good work now, or it will all have been for nothing. You deserve better!

The second pay cycle is difficult but not intolerable. You still require discipline and effort so you don't regress and undo all the hard work you put into everything you've just created.

Stay committed to the plan. You can do this!

Your Third Pay Cycle

For a lot of people, this pay is the tipping point. The point where you'll either keep going and make sustainable changes in your life or give in and go back to the way it was.

This pay cycle is probably the most important of them all.

It's crucial to continue with the plan and reinforce the positive habits you're creating to sustain your financial house long-term.

Your third pay cycle is where you positively reinforce and associate pleasure with your new habit.

You can see that your Catastrophe Account is growing, and it feels good to know that if any emergency happens, you're covered.

Hone Your Habits

You can see that your Household Expenses Account is taking care of your daily bills and they're all being paid on time.

You can see that your debt is reducing slowly but surely.

You can see that the plan is working, and it has all been worth it.

(Can I just say that I am so proud of you for getting this far!)

Think back to the pain and unhappiness you were feeling in the first pay cycle when the gremlin was trying to get you to blow your Splurge Account on one item. It was hard to resist. It was hard to say no. But you did it, and you should be proud of yourself.

The great news is that this stage is where your new habits start integrating into your lifestyle. It's becoming part of who you are, not what you do.

You're transitioning from someone who wasn't good with money to someone who has their financial ducks lined up and manages them like a pro. Instead of dreading payday and stressing over how you're going to pay the bills, you get excited because you're watching your money disburse into your accounts.

Now, a word of warning…

This is also the part where you can start to feel like you've got this all covered. You've got your budget. You've got your pay disbursed into your accounts. Everything is ticking over nicely. You think, 'I deserve a bit of a reward for all the hard work, so I'm not going to put that money into the Catastrophe Account. I'm going to leave it in my Splurge Account and treat myself to something special. I've earnt it!!'

This is your old habit trying to get back in control. Resist it at all costs!!!!

Yes, you've done amazing to get this far.

Yes, you've got some momentum.

Yes, you're starting to see results.

No, you don't want to stop!

If you stop now, you'll undo all the good work you've put in to get here.

Chances are, you'll think hard about starting again, but you probably won't. And if you do, you'll have to go back to the 'Your First Pay Cycle' stage and start all over again. Remember how that felt? You don't want to go there.

So this doesn't happen to you, let's look at some ways that we can make your new, amazing money habits stick.

Make it Stick

They say it takes 28 days to create a new habit and 90 days to make it a permanent lifestyle change.

While you've done an excellent job creating your new habit, now, when the rubber hits the road and temptation is sitting on your shoulder, what you do next is crucial.

Hone Your Habits

Here are some ideas on how you can make your habits stick:

Make it visual: Print something that inspires you and stick it on your fridge. It could be a motivational quote that helps you to keep going, a copy of your budget that keeps you engaged, or one of those thermometers that charities use when they're on a fundraising drive. Whatever it is, print it out, stick it on the fridge (or the back of your toilet door, or your bedside table so you see it first thing in the morning, or all three!). Wherever it will have the biggest impact, stick it up because this, to the exclusion of almost everything else, is what will turn your life around.

Know your excuses: These are the things that will sabotage your success. They're the bombs that will blow up all the hard work you've put in. 'But I need to…' 'But I have to…' 'I really must…' You know them. Intimately. Once you hear them in your mind, stop yourself mid-thought and choose the path you're on. Stopping your thoughts midway stops your mind from completing the old pattern that led you to your old habits. You have nice, shiny new habits that you're adopting that make your life a lot sweeter.

Set yourself up for success: Make time once a week, once a fortnight, and eventually once a month to keep track of and review your plan. Is it working? How are the numbers? Does something need to change? What can I tweak to make this even better? Being on the front foot keeps you engaged, motivated, and excited when you see the results of your efforts.

Commit to 30 days at a time: If you think of what happened in the last 90 days, you might be forgiven for being a little overwhelmed. There's a lot going on in your life right now. So breaking things down into more manageable timeframes helps keep the overwhelm under control and keep you on track. Every

30 days, you'll be cementing your new habits more and more. If you can make it through the initial three phases, you can make it through the next 30 days. A month is a good block of time to commit to a change since it easily fits into your calendar.

Get a buddy: We have a whole community of women who are going through and have gone through what you're experiencing. Finding someone who will go along with you and keep you motivated when you feel like quitting is key. If you don't have someone in your friend group or family, jump into our community and any one of us will be your buddy—myself included!

It's Your Turn

Creating positive money habits is like putting the special sauce on your burger. It just tastes better. Once you've established your habits, you'll look back and wonder how you ever managed your money before.

- ☐ Commit to your first three pay cycles and really give them everything you've got.
- ☐ Adopt one or two of the 'make it stick' strategies.
- ☐ Get yourself a buddy.
- ☐ Most importantly—if you fall off the wagon, get right back on. Start again. We have more about this coming up in a later chapter—Fashion Your First-Aid Kit.

CHAPTER TEN

Take Your Time

Think back to our formula:

A plan plus good, positive habits, over time, creates a new way of life.

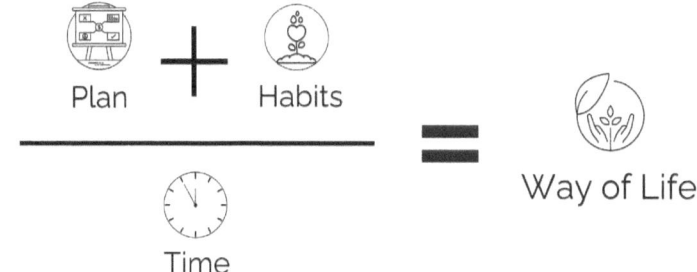

We're up to part three of the formula—time.

While the strategies I've shared with you in this book will work, they're not a magic pill or silver bullet. You won't wake up tomorrow morning and have a sparkling new life with zero debt and thousands of dollars stashed away in your Savvy Smile Account.

What you'll have is a solid plan and good financial habits.

It takes time for all of this to happen.

It takes time to pay off your debts.

It takes time to build your nest egg.

It takes time to get back on your feet.

But, honey, you have the time, even if it doesn't feel like it right now.

Overnight Success Takes Time

It was Jeff Bezos, founder of Amazon, who said, "Overnight success takes about 10 years."

Changing your money situation can be difficult. Let's be honest; it's really hard work a lot of the time. I'm not saying this to scare you, put you off, or make this harder. I'm saying this because it's the honest truth.

I don't want to sit here and say, '*Here's your plan, go forth and build your wealth*' like some evangelistic preacher with a congregation of starving and thirsty people desperate for someone to show them the light.

It doesn't work that way. But you already know that.

Forget about shortcuts. Forget about get-rich-quick schemes. They simply don't work.

What does work, however, are consistent steps repeated payday after payday until you see results. I'll use this analogy to demonstrate my point…

You decide one day that you want a tree in your front yard. The sun beams down in the afternoon, making the front room hot and uncomfortable. A big shady tree there will make a whole lot of difference. So, you plant a seed in your garden. You make sure it's in the perfect position so that when it grows, it won't have anything obstructing it. You water it and say a little prayer, hoping it'll grow big quickly. You wake up the next morning depressed and upset because there isn't a whole tree there providing shade to your front room.

Now, I know I'm being a bit ridiculous with this story. We all know that you won't have a mature tree in your garden the day after you plant a seed.

But I think it's a good illustration of what happens with our money, and I think it's probably one of the reasons why most people fall off the 'money wagon' and go back to the hustle and grind they used to have every payday.

The good news here is that if you get it right, managing your money will be one of the most rewarding things you'll do in your lifetime, and for me, it's been life-changing.

Gary Keller, author of the book *The One Thing*, says,

When you see someone who has a lot of knowledge, they learnt it over time. When you see someone who has a lot of skills, they developed them over time. When you see someone who has done a lot, they accomplished it over time. When you see someone who has a lot of money, they earned it over time.

So, if you're prepared to forget about luck and silver bullets, you'll see that, over time, you'll have the lifestyle and the happiness you truly wish for.

How Do You Eat Your Elephant?

Desmond Tutu once said, "There is only one way to eat an elephant, and that is one bite at a time."

What he meant by this is that everything in life that seems daunting, overwhelming and even impossible can be accomplished gradually by taking just one step at a time.

Over the last two to three decades, I've been studying human behaviour and why people do what they do. I have a weird fascination with people-watching. I find human beings strange creatures and, oftentimes, difficult to understand. (Is it just me, or do other people feel the same way?)

One of the things I've been really interested in is how successful people actually become successful. I've been fascinated by this because, as they say, "Success leaves clues," and success is on my bucket list. I'm not talking about that crazy Forbes 100 list or who's the richest person in Australia in 2021. I can never see myself as one of them. It's not who I am. I'm more interested in the 'average' person and how they become 'above-average' (does that make me weird? I don't know).

Take Your Time

One of the strategies I've seen over and over again and used in my own life is the Domino Strategy.

Remember, as a kid, we would create those long, windy snakes of dominos on the lounge room floor and fight over who was going to be the one to tip over the first domino. There would be screams of blue murder if you knocked them over early, or it wasn't your turn. The joy came in watching them all fall over one after the other. Then, setting them up to do it again. Fun times…

The Domino Strategy is simple, and I believe it will work for you too.

First, start small so that you can easily knock over the first domino. This could be doing your money audit so that you know your numbers. It takes about an hour to do and gives you a whole lot of peace of mind when you know what's coming in and going out. From there, you can make better decisions.

Second, put the dominos in just the right sequence so that each small step makes the next bigger step possible. The second step here could be to declutter your money. Think about what has slipped through the cracks and just leaks out of your account every month because you forgot about that subscription or you haven't watched that Pay-TV channel in almost a year.

The key to making this work is a sequence. Creating a plan to have $10,000 in your Catastrophe Account is great, but if you're drowning in debt and your interest rates cause your financial planner to go pale in the face, you may have the cart before the horse.

Trying to build up your savings is a great idea, and I strongly encourage you to do so, but if it's at the wrong time, it's basically the same as taking the wrong step. The dominos won't fall, and if you fail to reach your goal, there's a really good chance you'll quit.

Verne Harnish, co-founder of *Entrepreneurs' Organisation*, says, "Your job is to find that front domino, that number one thing that, if you could accomplish, will knock over the other ninety-eight and get more done than the other ninety-eight combined."

If you're stuck knowing where to start, ask yourself this question:

> *What is the one thing I can do to make everything else easier or unnecessary?*

Knock down that first domino, and you'll be well on your way to having a rich and fulfilling life.

Managing Your Overwhelm

If you've read this far (and I really hope you have), you might be thinking, gosh, there's a lot to do. I don't know if I can do it all.

You're not alone in thinking this.

We've all had times when it feels like our to-do list is piled so high that we can barely see the top of it. Or when your responsibilities are weighing on you so heavily that you can hardly breathe.

Just when you get one thing ticked off your list, another three take its place. It can feel like being hit by wave after wave at the beach.

There can also be a physical reaction to feeling overwhelmed. You can feel a tightening of the chest, headaches, or difficulty remembering things. And this doesn't help to get everything done, does it?

Hopefully, these things aren't happening to you all the time. But if you're feeling the bite of the overwhelm bug, here are a couple of things you can do to clear your mind and take some of the pressure off.

Write everything down: Sometimes, the best way to clear your head is to get everything down on paper. I remember doing this with a client a few years ago. When we finished dumping everything out of their mind, we ended up with a to-do list that was six pages long. Now, hopefully, this won't be the case for you, but by writing everything down, you take those feelings of overwhelm and the associated physical and mental symptoms and turn them into something quantifiable.

Everything from personal appointments, bills to be paid, work deadlines, and anything else that's running around your mind or possibly keeping you awake at night. Once they're listed on paper, you have a much better chance of making sense of them.

Get Started: Overwhelm can keep you stuck and paralysed, and the longer you stay in this space, the worse it can potentially become. Once you have written everything down, choose one or two small things you can get done or delegate immediately. This will give you a sense of progress and get some of the 'low-hanging fruit' taken care of. Then, it's a matter of tackling some of the bigger things. The Domino Strategy will help here.

Breathe: I know it's a bit of a cliché; however, stopping what you're doing and taking a few long, slow breaths that fill your lungs all the way into your diaphragm will help you calm your mind and centre your body. When you notice that your stress levels are rising and you're starting to feel anxious, come back to your breathing and spend a few moments getting centred again. Then, you can crack on with your list so you'll be more productive and get more accomplished.

Stay In Your Lane (It's not about other people—we're all running our own race)

There are several different interpretations of 'Stay in Your Lane.' One is an admonishment that suggests that one person doesn't understand another's situation due to a lack of knowledge. Another is basically 'stick to what you're good at'—you do you, and I'll do me.

But we're going to look at this a little bit differently (and a whole lot nicer).

It's so easy to compare yourself to other people and their achievements and successes. When you see your friends or neighbours go on that overseas trip they've been planning for years, it's easy to get wrapped up in their excitement and lunge for the credit card and blow it up on purchases to make you feel better.

Stay in your lane is a way of staying hyper-focused on yourself and your journey and not concentrating or comparing yourself to how other people are doing.

When you compare yourself to others, there are only two possible thoughts you can have:

1. They're better than us
2. We're better than them

Neither of which is helpful nor will move you closer to achieving your goals.

The other thing to take into consideration is that if you're constantly checking what other people are doing and focusing on their success and accomplishments, your attention is not on your pathway, and you'll fall over (it's not a *might* fall; it's a *will* fall). You're not watching where you're going; you'll end up going in the wrong direction and have to start again.

If you find yourself noticing that people are 'passing' you, remember that you don't have to react. Maybe you'll pass them later, or maybe not. But you need to be running the best race that you possibly can because, at the end of the day, you're not competing with them. You're competing with yourself. This is your journey, and your goal is to be better today than you were yesterday.

For me, this is one thing that I still have to remind myself to do. Whenever those thoughts pop into my mind, I make a conscious effort to remind myself that I'm in my own lane. I'm doing my thing. I'm on track to achieve the success that I want.

And so are you!

It's Your Turn

You know that turning your financial situation around will take some time. Once you get your head around that, you relieve some of the pressure and get clearer about your next steps.

☐ Create your Domino Strategy
☐ Manage your overwhelm
☐ Run your own race

CHAPTER ELEVEN

Live Your Life

For some reason, I keep hearing Bon Jovi's *It's My Life* in my mind every time I think about this chapter. The lyrics of the song somehow jump into my brain and end up staying there on repeat for hours, if not days.

It's become a silent anthem in my life (now that's embarrassing!!), but it's so true. Most of the great songs are born from truth, and this one is no different.

As a teenager in the 80s, with my big, permed hair, shoulder pads, and ra-ra skirts, I was all that and then some.

That was a lifetime ago. But I remember thinking that I could be and do anything. I felt that there were no limitations. That anything was possible. The sky was the limit.

Enter my husband, and my life went down a totally different path from the one I thought I would go down. Not that I regret it. Somehow, through all the dysfunction of our marriage and divorce, we have managed to raise four amazing children who are, to this day, my greatest achievements in life and continue to be my world. I make no apologies for that.

I feel like my life has taken a huge detour, and now I'm back to that place in my teens, minus the big hair, shoulder pads, and short skirts, of course. But I'm back to living my life. I'm a little bit older and a little bit wiser, somewhat bumped and bruised, but excited about life nonetheless.

I'm in the second phase of my life, the one that Dr. Wayne Dyer calls the 'Afternoon of Our Life,' and I'm ok with that. A lot of the struggle and the 'crap' from the first half of my life is over. Now, it's my turn, and I'm going to make the most of every single second.

New Beginnings

One of the great things that comes from deciding to change your financial situation is that it's a new beginning. Even though it may not feel like it, it *is* the next chapter of your life—coming ready or not.

This fresh start is an opportunity to redefine what financial success means to you. It's a chance to shed old beliefs and habits that no longer serve you and embrace new practices that align with your goals. As you begin on this journey, remember that every small step you take contributes to a larger transformation.

Embracing new beginnings allows you to cultivate a mindset of possibility and resilience. It's about recognising that your past doesn't dictate your future; instead, you have the power to create a life that reflects your values and dreams. With each decision, you're not just managing money—you're crafting a lifestyle that prioritises your well-being and happiness.

As you navigate this transition, it's normal to feel a mix of excitement and uncertainty. But with every choice you make, you're building a foundation for a brighter future. Celebrate your progress, no matter how small, and give yourself permission to grow. This is your moment to shine, explore, and thrive in your own unique way.

There's a whole new, exciting, enticing, beautiful, expansive world waiting for you to join. You just need to take the first step. Commit to it right here, right now. Say to yourself:

> *I am here.*
> *Despite all the hurt, pain, and setbacks, I am here.*
> *Despite all the knockers, non-believers, and naysayers, I am here.*
> *Despite all the challenges, obstacles, and mountains I have climbed, I am here.*
> *I am here, I am breathing, I am loving, and I am living.*
> *I am here, and I am making my life mean something.*
> *I am here, and I am doing crazy things I never knew I could do.*
> *I am here, and I am living larger than I thought possible.*
> *I am here, I am growing, I am changing, and I am up-levelling all areas of my life.*
> *I am here, and I am loving all parts of myself and learning to accept all that I am.*
> *I am here.*

Repeat this every morning when you wake up and every night before you go to sleep. I wrote this passage in my journal the morning before I wrote this chapter. It poured out of me. I didn't have to stop or think; it just tumbled out of my mind and onto the pages of my journal. Tears streamed down my face as I wrote it. It was cleansing my heart and renewing my belief in myself.

You're here. You're more than you realise, and you're about to turn a corner that will change the direction of your life forever.

Discernment

Discernment is a word that I discovered years ago, and it's something that took a little while to get my head around and even longer to put into practice.

Discernment is the ability to judge well.

Now, I always thought I was a good judge of character, people, situations, and events. Turns out I'm not so good at it.

I'm one of those people that takes everything at face value. It is what it is.

But the older I'm getting, I'm finding that it's more and more important to become discerning.

In its simplest form, discernment is the ability to decide between truth and error, right and wrong, possible and impossible. It's the process of making careful distinctions in our thinking.

To me, discernment is about making inspired choices. Sometimes, we're able to make spontaneous decisions like chocolate or vanilla ice cream. Other times, the choices we need to make require deep thought and consideration, like whether I'll buy a brand new or a used car.

Live Your Life

When it comes to being good with money and doing the right thing with your finances, the temptation is to think we just need to know more information and more facts. However, knowledge or information alone is rarely what stops us from enjoying the success we want or achieving our goals.

If just having all the information was enough for us to make great decisions, everyone would have all they need. The question then becomes, how do you make good financial decisions if knowledge alone isn't enough?

To improve your ability to make good money decisions, you need two things:

1. *Clarity on your values and priorities*
2. *Understanding of your current financial reality*

Good financial decisions come from understanding where these two things meet. Choices about how to use your money will be easier if you know what's truly important to you.

What are your core values?

What really matters to you?

Why are you trying to improve your financial situation?

More money on its own is not a true goal. It's what the money allows you to do in your life that's key.

If you align your spending with what's most important, keeping to your budget becomes much easier. If you know what you want to save for, you can suddenly find more motivation to grow your savings.

When you struggle to make good financial decisions, making things 'right' or 'wrong' won't help either.

Seeing something as right or wrong can hit us in the core of our being and cause us to judge ourselves accordingly—I always get it right or I always get it wrong.

Instead, ask yourself, 'Does this work for me?' or, 'Does this not work for me?'

Determining what works and what doesn't comes down to your financial reality and goals, not whether you're a good, bad, smart, or not-so-smart person.

When you approach your financial decisions in this way, you become more discerning about your choices and, therefore, more empowered.

Remember, the future is unknown, and from the present moment, you really have no idea how each of your decisions will play out 5, 15 or 30 years from now. So when you have to make a difficult choice, and you're not sure which path to take, consider what choice most aligns with the person you want to be and the lifestyle you want to live.

Boundaries (Protect Them)

Setting and maintaining boundaries is one of the most important things we can do for our mental and emotional health. Boundaries are a commitment to respect ourselves and our priorities.

We usually associate boundaries with the people in our life. If you don't respect each other's boundaries, the relationship can become strained or toxic. If both parties have clearly defined expectations that are respected, then the relationship is more likely to thrive.

But what about our relationship with money?

Having clear and defined financial boundaries leads to a healthy relationship with money, which helps you accomplish your financial goals.

For example, you may have a goal to pay off your credit card. A boundary you might establish is to put your own financial needs before others. Instead of paying for lunch when you catch up with your bestie, you could split the bill and only pay for the food you've eaten.

No one wants to receive a present from you knowing that the cost of that present means you have to eat two-minute noodles until your next payday. Setting a limit on birthday presents will sometimes mean that you have to be more creative with your spending, but when you hand that gift over knowing that it comes from your heart instead of your wallet, you'll both win.

Setting financial boundaries is about protecting your well-being now and in the future.

It's important to make sure that your perception and relationship with money boundaries are healthy. If you view boundaries as limitations, then it will be more difficult to follow through on them. However, if you view money boundaries as a healthy tool to ensure you're better positioned to meet your goals, then you'll see the endless opportunities ahead.

To honour your money boundaries, you may need to have a conversation with your nearest and dearest to explain that you're focusing on your financial matters and need to change how you've been spending your money until now. Talking about money is often difficult, but communicating honestly and effectively is key. People can't respect your boundaries if they don't know what they are, so open and transparent communication is vital.

Putting your financial needs above others means that you'll be able to give freely and generously once your cup is full. And that's a fabulous feeling.

Enjoy It!

For so many of us, achieving a goal is a great thing but not something we stop and celebrate. Our lives have become so busy that we swiftly move on to the next challenge and the next challenge and the next challenge without acknowledging what we've just accomplished.

Do this often enough, and you'll miss out on some really amazing celebrating!

So, what have you achieved?

I want you to stop doing what you're doing and just sit for a minute. Like, an actual minute. Right now. This minute.

Put the book down, sit for a minute, and think about all the things you've achieved in your life. From coming first at sports day in primary school to your first kiss, moving out from home, buying your first car, getting married, having babies, getting your first job, earning your degree, and getting your license.

Take a minute to do that now. I'll be right here when you get back, I promise.

Live Your Life

Tick Tock (yes, there are sixty tick tocks there which should equal a minute).

What did you notice? What memories came up for you? Did anything bring up your emotions?

I know it does for me when I stop and remember all the things I've accomplished in my life. Things like:

- Homing a rescue cat was something I've wanted to do for years, so I adopted Flossy.
- Living alone was one of the scariest things I've ever thought of, yet here I am, not just living but thriving on my own.
- Watching my oldest child become a parent filled my heart with a new love I hadn't known before.
- Holding my grandbabies in my arms for the first time is something I fail to describe due to the limitations of language, yet it fills my heart with unlimited joy and love.
- Watching my twins step in for their dad, who couldn't make it to our daughter's wedding and walk their sister down the aisle, made my heart swell with pride so much that my eyes started leaking.
- Writing a book, starting a business, and being a figure on social media are things I never thought I would be doing, and yet here I am.

Taking a moment to take stock of your life and all the things you've accomplished is so important when it comes to achieving more goals. Your mind and body need to know what success feels like. When you hurry through to the next goal and the next goal, you miss this vital step in the process.

So, when you achieve a milestone or a goal, particularly when you make small sacrifices to get ahead financially, make sure that you enjoy the moment and celebrate. It makes achieving your next goal so much sweeter.

It's Your Turn

It's so easy to get stuck in the whirlpool of emotions that can take hold of us. But if you have the strength and motivation to turn your attention onto something else that brings more happiness and joy to your life, your next chapter can be your best one yet.

- ☐ It's your new beginning, grab hold and make it count.
- ☐ Be discerning with your choices.
- ☐ Set money boundaries to protect your financial future.
- ☐ Enjoy and celebrate the milestones you've achieved.

CHAPTER TWELVE

Fashion Your First-Aid Kit

I think it's safe to say there will be an occasion when you fall off the financial wagon. You may have forgotten about a bill, gone on a spending spree and spent too much money or not stuck to your budget and ended up having to take all the money out of your Catastrophe Account and deep dive into your Savvy Smile Account to cover yourself.

People who suffer a financial setback are often described as feeling shock, fear, regret, and sometimes anger, often at themselves. Their health has sometimes suffered, and they've found it hard to move on.

What you do when this happens is just as important as any other step we've looked at in this book.

Packing it in and going home with your tail between your legs to hide and never show your face in public again is very tempting.

Picking yourself up after a financial setback takes courage and determination, which you have in spades.

Oops…

This may be shocking to learn, but I have inherited the ability to catastrophise situations (thanks, Mum x). Now, this may seem funny, and a lot of the time it is (afterward, of course), but sometimes I can go completely overboard and experience a catastrophic reaction to a minor error in judgment.

And I don't think I'm alone.

It's common to feel like you're never going to get it when you're learning something new. We start with unconscious incompetence, which is where we don't know what we don't know. Yes, ignorance can sometimes be bliss.

Then we go to conscious incompetence. We become aware that we don't know how to do something, which prompts us to find an answer (this is probably why you're reading this book).

We transition into conscious competence once we learn the steps we need to take. This is where we have to consciously think about what we need to do and when we need to do it.

Then, finally, we move into unconscious competence, where we no longer have to think about it. It just happens at an unconscious level.

When you're trying to master something new, you're in conscious competence, where it's extremely common to make a mistake. We watch this happen when our babies are learning to walk. They fall over, then get back up and try again. Same thing when we're learning to drive or learning a new sport or a new skill.

If you blew out your Splurge Account in the first few days after your payday and you don't have enough money to get through until the next payday, you made an error, but you're not going to die because of it.

It doesn't mean that you're bad with money. It doesn't mean that you're never going to get this right. It doesn't mean you should throw in the towel and be financially destitute for the rest of your life.

What it **does** mean is that you'll have to postpone your plans to catch up with your friends for lunch on Saturday and instead eat out of your freezer and pantry for the next week until payday comes around and your funds are replenished.

It's important to make sure that if you do take a tumble or go completely splat on the floor, you're looking at the situation as factually as possible. You made a mistake. You're not a financial dummy. You'll get it right next time (especially if you've had to eat leftovers out of your freezer for the last nine days).

Be Kind to Yourself

When we mess up, we tend to overanalyse that mistake for hours, and the anxiety and stress can be debilitating.

For me personally, making mistakes and dealing with those mistakes has been incredibly hard my entire life. I have always had

Saving Myself

a 'good girl complex' and chased perfection relentlessly. So, the idea of making a mistake or getting it wrong was truly unbearable.

When I was younger (and if I'm honest, even up until my 30s), I had no compassion for myself and would spiral quickly into self-loathing. I was that kid who couldn't be consoled if I made a mistake or got into trouble. I was harder on myself than my parents, my teachers, or any other adult could ever be.

Learning self-compassion and how to be kind to myself wasn't easy. I had to undo decades of believing I had to be perfect to be loved, and anything less would mean I was a worthless human being.

Being kind to yourself means sitting with yourself, acknowledging how you feel, truly letting yourself feel it, and then saying to yourself what you would say to your bestie. It's about reminding yourself that it's ok to feel this way, that you're not alone and, most importantly, that there's growth in this mistake.

Being kind to yourself is like being your own best friend. Take some of the advice and compassion you give to others and give it to yourself.

It's key to allow yourself to recognise that you're only human, surrounded by millions of other humans who are trying their best and sometimes failing too.

Living my life with a 'good girl complex' meant I sought permission to do almost everything. I had to know if what I wanted to do was allowed or not so that I didn't get it wrong.

Giving myself permission to get it wrong was a huge step forward as an adult and allowed me the space and freedom to not only breathe but fail in a way that meant I was still a good girl.

Fashion Your First-Aid Kit

So, I want you to give yourself permission to get it occasionally wrong. Remember that even the greatest financial minds of our times get it wrong now and again.

I want you to say out loud:

> I, (insert your name), hereby give myself permission to get things wrong occasionally so that I can learn and do things better next time.

Giving myself permission to fall over and stumble has been a huge change in my life. It's given me the confidence to be able to make a mistake, even completely fail, and then get up and go again.

It has allowed me to stop giving myself such a hard time and be as kind and forgiving to myself as I am to other people.

Review Your Position

Once you overcome the emotions you've experienced with this setback, it's time to get to work and review your position.

No matter what caused your stumble, be honest with yourself about your situation because this is the only way you can move forward and regain ground as quickly as possible.

Ask yourself, where am I sitting right now? What's the impact of this setback?

Here are a few things you can do:

- Go back to your numbers. Have they changed? Do they look different now, or are they the same?

- Review your budget. Do you need to change anything? Is it still going to work the way it is?
- Reassess your debt position. Has this had an impact on your debt? Have you gone backward? Have you stayed the same?

Gather the information you need to assess your situation so that you know exactly what you're dealing with. This way, you can recover and get back on track.

Make An Adjustment

Now that you have reviewed your position, you may realise you need to adjust your financial plan.

It's important to understand what you have to do next to make sure you're still aligned with your goals. What changes do you need to make now to help you get there?

Depending on the size of the setback, you can make a small tweak or completely rework some areas of the plan.

This is the time for action. Don't sit back and wish, hope, and pray that it will get better. It won't until you do something about it.

Go Again

Now that you've corrected your mistake, it's time to get back to the plan and go again.

It's even more important to let go of your mistake. You have acknowledged it, licked your wounds, reviewed your situation, and adjusted your plan accordingly. You're back on track to achieve your goals.

You've done everything you can now to help you learn from your mistakes and work towards a brighter future, so there's no point hanging onto the past. You deserve to be free from the guilt and to give yourself some grace and love again.

Remember, we all make financial mistakes. What you do after you've made them makes all the difference. Will you keep digging yourself a bigger hole, or will you recognise the error of your ways and do something about it?

Your financial mistakes don't have to define your future.

It's Your Turn

Let's be honest, we all make mistakes. No exceptions. But as the saying goes, it's what you do after you've made the mistake that's the difference that will make the difference.

- ☐ Be nice to yourself
- ☐ Review your position
- ☐ Make the necessary adjustments
- ☐ Get back to the plan

Conclusion

As we've touched on many times in this book, coming back from being a Hot Money Mess can be one of the most challenging times in your life. For some women, it doesn't take long to turn things around. For others, it's a journey that takes years of effort and determination.

I hope you can move past the worry and stress of your past decisions sooner rather than later. If you feel stuck, I hope this book gives you some hope and pushes you in the right direction.

I've always found that starting something new or diving into a fresh project brings a sense of optimism and excitement. It shifts the focus from the past to what's possible in the future. For you, it might be taking control of your finances.

I promise that you'll feel more confident and ready to embrace what's ahead over time. You'll find yourself becoming your 'new self'—wiser, stronger, and ready to make choices with a clearer vision. And that's an amazing place to be.

Saving Myself

Only You Can Make a Difference to Your Future

I think that the worst thing you could do right now is put this book back on the shelf. Honestly. The worst thing.

However, the best thing you could do would be to put the steps you have learnt in this book into action.

There's a harsh reality I'm going to share with you now. You're the only one who can make a real difference in your future. Not me. Not your mum. Not your bestie. Not your husband, ex-husband or your partner. Just you. Only you.

It's time, right now, for you to get up, get going and create some action in your financial life. You've gone through each chapter of this book and have created the perfect plan. It's tailor-made just for you.

You've created some positive money and behaviour habits that will support your plan. You also know this isn't a silver bullet and will take some time to perfect, but you have the time and motivation.

All you need to do now is make it happen.

If you're feeling scared, go back to chapter one and read the section on fear again.

If you're not sure you have what it takes, go back to chapter three and re-read the whole chapter. It's time to change your story.

There's nothing you can tell me, no excuse, and no reason that'll convince me you cannot do this. Because I believe you can. But only you can make a difference to your future.

I choose you. Who do you choose?

Conclusion

Money Won't Make You Happy—Being in Control of Your Money Will

Money won't buy you happiness. How often have you heard that saying, I wonder?

To some extent, it's true. You cannot go to the store and buy a kilo of happiness. "Oh and pop me in 300g of laugh out loud as well, will you?"

It just doesn't happen, does it?

Money won't buy you happiness. It can't. It won't. It never will. But it will buy you something that's absolutely priceless.

Money can allow you to hire a cleaner to come into your home once a week, fortnight, or month, which will free up half a day that you can spend doing something you love. And you'll be supporting a local business by becoming one of their clients. It's a win-win for both of you.

Money can allow you to buy steak instead of sausages at the grocery store and cook a delicious meal for yourself that really makes you smile. Or even better, allow you to get takeaway when you're tired at the end of the day. Or even better still, treat yourself to a night out at your favourite restaurant. You have options now.

Money can allow you to go on that trip of a lifetime. The one you've been dreaming about since you were a little kid. For me, this is three months living in a village in France.

Money can free up your time so that you can spend it with your loved ones, which is priceless.

It's true, money won't make you happy, but being in control of your money and not being hog-tied by debt and debilitated by rising interest rates is a freedom that few enjoy. But it's available to you right now.

Financial Control = Self Worth

There's something funny that happens to the women I help when they get their finances under control. Their confidence increases, and their self-worth gets a massive boost!

It was Henry Ford who said, *"If you think you can or you think you can't, you're right."*

Once you realise that you *can* be in control of your finances, your self-worth, self-esteem, and self-confidence go up dramatically.

Your perception of yourself and how worthy you think you are directly correlates with your net worth. Deciding not to buy a pair of shoes because you begin to see money as an act of nourishing yourself shows that you're seeing yourself as worthy of keeping the money you make.

The key here is seeing yourself as a long-term investment. Taking care of yourself financially is one of many ways to ensure you're ok so you can be there for others.

Commit to The Plan

Being in control of your money can be an aphrodisiac. It can give you a high that's addictive. It can make you stand taller. It can help you do more. It can allow you to experience more freedom than you realise.

Conclusion

For too long, money has been your master. It has been the one that has controlled you. It has determined how you live your life—drowning in debt and living on scraps.

But not anymore; money is now one of the assets you manage well and it works to give you the freedoms you so deserve.

All you need to do is remember our formula...

A plan, plus good positive habits, over time,

equals a new way of life.

You've got the plan. You've got the good habits. You've got the time. All you need to do now is put everything into action and create a life that fills your heart and soul with love and abundance.

Stay in Contact

This book has been equal parts a labour of love and a huge undertaking for me to write. Talking openly about things we're meant to keep private hasn't always been easy. I feel like I've been through my own therapy session in the process.

Saving Myself

Although it's not always easy to share some of the intimate details of my life, I feel that I can trust you with my story.

I would love for you to stay in contact with me. Visit my website – www.jobaker.com.au where I share even more information about living life as the Queen of Choices. I'd love to see you there.

Or if you'd like a more personal conversation, you're always welcome to reach out to me at hello@jobaker.com.au.

I hope this is not the end for us. I hope to speak to you real soon.

Take care of yourself, and remember that you're the Queen of Choices, too, now. Anything is possible.

Jo xx

Do Not Allow Your Fire To Go Out

"Do not allow your fire to go out, spark by irreplaceable spark in the hopeless swamps of the not quite, the not yet and the not at all. Do not let the hero in your soul perish in lonely frustration for the life you deserved and have never been able to reach. The world you desire can be won. It exists. It is real. It is possible. It is yours."

~ Ayn Rand ~

Your Journey Continues

THE 28-DAY SAVING MYSELF MONEY CHALLENGE

As you start this transformative journey, I want to ensure you have all the support you need to turn the insights from this book into real-life actions. That's why I'm excited to invite you to join the 28-Day Saving Myself Money Challenge, exclusively for readers of this book.

This challenge is designed to help you apply the principles you've learnt through an easy-to-navigate online portal. Over 28 days, you'll have daily prompts and reminders to guide you toward becoming unstoppable in the pursuit of your dream life.

And the best part? This challenge is completely free! It's my gift to you for taking this important step toward a brighter financial future. I can't wait to see you inside, supporting you every step of the way.

Saving Myself

To access the challenge, simply visit jobaker.com.au/28-day, and enter your name, email address, and receipt number. Once you do, you'll gain access to my online portal filled with all the lessons, downloads, and information you need to get the most out of this book.

Remember, making it happen is a choice. So choose it!

About the Author

Jo Baker is on a mission to empower women to embrace managing their money with confidence and live a life that feels true to who they are, no matter their circumstances.

Jo helps women rebuild their confidence from the inside out through her community and programs, starting with their finances. She teaches women how to become their own financial expert, freeing them to spend more time doing what they love.

Jo simplifies what can often feel overwhelming. She breaks down managing money into easy, actionable steps that are rooted in simple maths and practical life skills—no jargon or complicated theories.

With her straightforward approach, women can see real results quickly, and step into a new way of life. Jo says, "You don't have to be a financial whizz to be financially savvy. No matter your age or situation, small imperfect steps will improve your financial position and, in turn, your overall well-being."

Jo's work is about more than just managing money—it's about helping women step into their full power, making decisions with confidence, and creating a life of financial independence. Her approach is designed to uplift and inspire, showing women they have everything they need within them to not only handle their finances but to thrive.

Jo is here to guide you toward a future where financial clarity gives you the freedom to live life on your own terms, with purpose and peace of mind.

Acknowledgements

There's no way I could have lived this life and travelled this journey on my own. These are just some of the women who have walked the path with me.

My mum, Rae. Everything I am is because of you. The limitations of the English language mean that I struggle to put into words how much you mean to me. But I never struggle to feel your love and support. It is always with me, regardless of where I am in this world.

My grandma, Doris, my nan, Josie, and my aunt, Val. They say it takes a village to raise a child. I couldn't have been in better hands. I love you.

My daughter, Gaby. I'm so incredibly proud of the woman you have become. Every day you make me smile and laugh. You were born into a family of incredible women. There is nothing you cannot do.

My granddaughters, Harlee and Hope. Your smiles melt my heart. Your laughter touches my soul. The strength and courage of the women who have come before you live within you. Fly amongst the eagles my darling girls.

Saving Myself

To Suskia, who has been my shoulder to cry on when life has beaten the hell out of me, my greatest advocate when I hit the highs and everything in between. Thank you for all the joy, happiness and laughter you have brought to my life for over 20 years. There's no one like you in this world. I love you to bits.

To Therese, I absolutely know that I wouldn't be doing this had it not been for you and that conversation we had at the coffee shop on Collins St. Your faith and belief in me, well before I could see it myself, has changed the course of my life. You are one in a million and I'm so grateful to have you as my friend.

To the team at Ultimate World Publishing, none of this would be possible without you. To Nat, Stu, Vivi, Julie, Rebecca, Nik and the whole team, you helped to make my dream of being a published author come true. Your support, encouragement and belief in me has never wavered. I wouldn't be where I am without you and I am forever grateful that you are in my world.

To my gorgeous coach Sarah Walton, from the other side of the world you have helped me bring my dream to life. You have held my hand and walked through my fears with me, been the cheerleader of my biggest game yet and the champion of my dreams. I will never be able to thank you enough for everything you've done for me.

To my community of exceptional women that I get to work with every day, I am honoured that you have chosen to walk the path with me. Together, we are recreating the face of women and finance which is leading to generational change. I wouldn't be where I am today without you.

Notes

Saving Myself

Notes

Saving Myself

Notes

Saving Myself

Notes

www.ingramcontent.com/pod-product-compliance
Lightning Source LLC
Chambersburg PA
CBHW021146080526
44588CB00008B/243